# Fleecie Pets

# Fleecie Pets

Cute and cuddly toys for babies and toddlers

Fiona Goble

NEW HOLLAND

First published in 2007 by
New Holland Publishers (UK) Ltd
London • Cape Town • Sydney • Auckland

Garfield House
86-88 Edgware Road
London W2 2EA
United Kingdom
www.newhollandpublishers.com

80 McKenzie Street
Cape Town 8001
South Africa

Level 1, Unit 4
14 Aquatic Drive
Frenchs Forest, NSW 2086
Australia

218 Lake Road
Northcote
Auckland
New Zealand

10 9 8 7 6 5 4 3 2 1

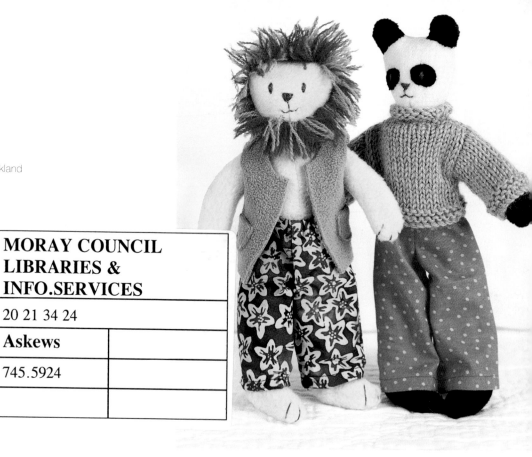

Text and project design copyright © 2007 Fiona Goble
Photographs copyright © 2007 New Holland Publishers (UK) Ltd
Copyright © 2007 New Holland Publishers (UK) Ltd

ISBN 978-1-84537-614-7

Editor: Ruth Hamilton
Design: Roland Codd
Photography: Shona Wood
Production: Hazel Kirkman
Editorial Direction: Rosemary Wilkinson

Reproduction by Colourscan, Singapore
Printed and bound by Craft Print International, Singapore

# Contents

# Introduction

This collection of soft and adorable fleecie creatures, each about 25 cm (10 in) tall, will appeal to soft toy and animal lovers of all ages.

They are made from soft polyester fleece which is readily available and reasonably priced, and are dressed in outfits made from the same fabric or from oddments of printed cottons and double knitting wools.

Unlike many soft toys, they are unbelievably quick and simple to make, and you only need basic sewing and knitting skills to achieve great results. There are no fiddly gussets or tiny limbs to sew on because each Fleecie Pet is made from just two main pieces. The feet and ears are part of the main body piece and are simply folded and stitched in place once the animal has been stuffed.

As well as full-size templates and instructions for making the 12 featured Fleecie Pets and their outfits, this book also includes details on making a wide range of accessories. There are also plenty of ideas for taking the concept a stage further in The Fleecie Pet Workshop, including how to customise your animal and even design your own creature.

I hope you enjoy browsing through this book and deciding which animal you want to make first. Above all, I hope you will have fun and be proud of your results!

Fiona Goble

# Tools and Materials

## TOOLS

Before you start making your first Fleecie Pet you will need some basic sewing and knitting equipment, some of which you will probably have already and other items you may need to buy.

### Access to a photocopier, thin card and sticky tape

The easiest and most accurate way to transfer your Fleecie Pet templates is to photocopy the templates onto thick paper or thin card. Alternatively, you can use a sheet of tracing paper. The body and head templates are separate so you will also need some sticky tape to fasten them together before cutting out (see page 11).

### Sewing machine and sewing machine needles (1)

You can easily sew your Fleecie Pets and clothes by hand but a sewing machine will make it much quicker. All you need is a machine that does basic running stitch, although one that also does zigzag stitch will be useful for giving a professional finish to some of the clothes. Your machine should be fitted with a needle suitable for medium weight fabrics. A standard European size 70 or 80 (US 11 or 12) needle is ideal. It's a good idea to have a few available as machine needles can bend or become blunt quite easily and you will need to replace them fairly often.

### Needles for hand sewing (2)

You will need three types of hand sewing needles to make your Fleecie Pets. These are a standard sewing needle, an embroidery needle and a tapestry needle.

You will need a standard sewing needle, (a 'sharp') for hand sewing your Fleecie Pets and clothes. Even if you are sewing by machine, you will need a hand sewing needle like this for sewing the animals' feet and ears, fixing the patches featured on some of the animals and closing the gap used for stuffing. A medium size needle is fine – choose one that it not so thin that it bends easily but not so thick that it is hard to push through your fabric.

To embroider your Fleecie Pet's features you will need an embroidery or crewel needle. This is a medium length sharp needle that has an eye large enough for you to thread embroidery thread.

For making up the Fleecie Pets' jumpers and knitted accessories, you will also need a tapestry needle. These are thick, blunt needles with an eye large enough to be threaded with knitting wool.

### Iron

You will need an iron when making the Fleecie Pets' clothes to press open seams, fix bonding web and appliqués, and giving a professional finish to some of the finished items.

### Water-soluble pen or quilter's pencil (3)

You will need a water-soluble pen or quilter's pencil to draw round the templates and to mark the toys' features before you embroider them. They work like ordinary pens or pencils but the marks are easily removed by spraying or dabbing with water. The pens usually come in bright blue and are the best option for marking lighter coloured fabrics. For darker fabrics, choose one of the pencils which come in a range of light colours, including white, yellow and blue. Water-soluble pens and quilter's pencils are widely available in craft and haberdashery shops, and through mail order companies and internet sites that supply accessories for patchwork and quilting.

### Ordinary pencil (4)

You will need a pencil for tracing the appliqué shapes featured on some of the clothes onto the backing paper of your bonding web (see page 10). A pencil is also useful for pushing the toy filling into the Fleecie Pets' limbs when you are stuffing them.

### Scissors (5)

Ordinary scissors are fine for cutting out your pattern paper but you will need a pair of good quality sewing scissors for cutting fabric. Make sure that you keep them strictly for cutting fabric as using them on paper or card will quickly blunt them.

### Dressmakers' pins (6)

You will need a small number of dressmakers' pins to pin your work together before basting or sewing. It is a good idea to use pins with coloured glass ends. These are much easier to see, and therefore less likely to get left in your work by mistake.

### Knitting needles and crochet hook (7)

To knit the Fleecie Pets' jumpers and some of the accessories you will need a pair of 3.75mm (US 5) knitting needles. For Spangles the Cat's handbag and the knitted cape in the Accessories section you will also need a 4mm (US 6) crochet hook.

### Row markers (8)

A set of row markers is useful to mark certain places in your work when knitting the Fleecie Pet jumpers. Alternatively, you can use some small safety pins.

### Safety pin (9)

You will need a small safety pin to thread the elastic cord through the waistbands of the Fleecie Pets' trousers, shorts and skirts.

## MATERIALS

All the materials you need to make the Fleecie Pets are readily available in dress fabric shops and haberdashery stores or from mail order and internet companies. The main fabric used for the Pets themselves is polyester fleece – sometimes called 'polar fleece'. This is the fabric used to make items such as fleece jumpers and hats. You will also need polyester toy filling to stuff your Fleecie Pets

and embroidery threads for their features. Depending on which animal you are making, you will also need different fabric for their clothes, knitting wools for jumpers and accessories, and a selection of trimmings. The exact materials needed to make each Fleecie Pet are given on the individual project pages.

### Fleece fabric (1, overleaf)

The Pets and some of the clothes and accessories are made from polyester fleece fabric. Fleece fabric comes in different thicknesses and finishes. It varies from smooth, thin fabrics used for lightweight tops to thick, shaggy fabrics used for winter jackets. Light to medium fleece is the ideal fabric for making Fleecie Pets as very thin fabrics tend to be too stretchy and thick fabrics are too bulky and difficult to work with.

Fleece fabric in a good range of neutral colours is available in many dress fabric shops. But don't worry if there isn't a good fabric shop in your area as fleece is also available at competitive prices by mail order or over the internet (see Suppliers page 95).

If you want an even greater choice of colours and textures, you could look at fleece clothing in budget clothing shops and in second hand shops. You could even transform your own old clothes into Fleecie Pets!

### Polyester filling (2, overleaf)

This 100% polyester filling is manufactured specially for stuffing soft toys, cushions and other handmade items. It is widely available in craft shops and haberdashery stores. Always check that the filling you are buying is marked safe and washable and that it conforms to safety standards.

### Plain and printed cottons (3, overleaf)

For many of the Fleecie Pets' clothes you will need small amounts of plain or printed fabrics in 100% cotton or cotton mixes (a blend of polyester and cotton). You don't need to use exactly the same fabric shown in the project, but for printed fabrics, small designs and prints work best. You can find these in dress fabric shops, craft shops, patchwork shops, and mail order and internet companies.

### Knitting wools (4, overleaf)

The Fleecie Pets' jumpers and knitted accessories are made from standard double knitting yarn. It is very important that you use good quality double knitting yarn that is at least 40% wool. Some cheaper acrylic yarns can be flat and heavy and will give disappointing results.

### Embroidery thread (5)

The Fleecie Pets' eyes, noses, mouths and paws are embroidered with 100% cotton stranded embroidery thread. This is made up of six strands that can be easily separated. For the projects in this book you will work with three strands. The colour used depends on the Fleecie Pet you are making and these details are included in the individual project pages. Black thread works well in many cases but for lighter fleece, dark grey or dark brown is best.

### Sewing thread (6)

Whether you are sewing with a machine or by hand, you will need standard sewing threads to match all your fabrics. Threads made from 100% polyester, often called 'all purpose' are widely available and come in a wide range of colours.

### Speciality fabrics (7)

For some of the Fleecie Pets you will need fabrics such as cotton knits (the sort of fabric used for T-shirts), polyester net (used to make dance skirts), acrylic sheepskin lining, and ripstop nylon (used to make lightweight rain gear). The precise requirements are given on the individual project pages. If you can't find the fabric you need in your local fabric shop, you can buy it by mail order or over the internet. Alternatively, you can recycle items from second hand clothes shops or even your own wardrobe.

### Elastic cord (8)

You will need narrow elastic cord to thread through the narrow waistbands of the Fleecie Pets' trousers, skirts and shorts. This is widely available and comes in black or white. As the elastic will not usually show, it doesn't really matter which colour you use.

### Bonding web (9)

For some of the clothing you will need a small amount of fusible bonding web to fasten the appliqués. Bonding web is a thin web of dry glue that is fixed on a paper backing. It is ironed onto the reverse side of the fabric. The shape for the appliqué is drawn on the paper backing with a normal pencil and then cut out. The backing can then be peeled off and the appliqué pressed in place with an iron. There are several brands of bonding web available and it is widely available in craft shops and haberdashery stores.

### Buttons and trimmings (10)

For some of the clothes and accessories you will need small buttons, snap fasteners and small amounts of ribbon. If you don't have these in your workbox, you can buy them in your local craft or haberdashery shop. Second hand shops are also a good source of buttons and sometimes other items, at very reasonable prices.

**Safety** It is very important that you do not give any Fleecie Pets with added extras such as buttons to children under three years old as these can be a choking hazard. All the Fleecie Pets and clothes can be adapted to suit younger children. For example, the buttons and snap fasteners on Rumble the Bear's dungarees can be omitted and the straps sewn to the bib of the dungarees instead. The button on Spangles the Cat's jumper can simply be omitted, as well as any pipe-cleaners that are used in the Pets.

# Techniques

## PREPARING YOUR TEMPLATES

All the Fleecie Pets in this book are made with the same body template – it is only the head templates that differ. The easiest way to prepare your template is to use a photocopier. Simply photocopy the body piece and the head piece of your choice (see pages 84–94) onto thick paper or thin card, cut them out and join them together at the neck edges with a small piece of sticky tape. If you don't have access to a photocopier, you can trace the body on a piece of tracing paper and trace the head of your choice in the correct position. You can then cut out a single pattern piece.

## TRANSFERRING YOUR TEMPLATE TO YOUR FABRIC

The easiest way to transfer your pattern is to hold the template firmly in position on the reverse side of your fabric and draw round it using a water-soluble pen or quilter's pencil. You can use the same pen or pencil to mark the position of the body dart. Simply poke the pen nib or pencil tip through the card template to mark the small circles – or make a hole in the template first using a large needle.

> **Tip** Whether you are shaping ears or feet or embroidering the face features or claws, secure your thread at the beginning and end of your work by making two or three tiny stitches into the side seam and pulling them tightly. These stitches will be virtually invisible. If you are using a dark embroidery thread on a light fabric, you may find it easier to secure your thread in a place where it will be hidden by the Fleecie Pet's clothes. For example, when embroidering the face features, secure the thread in the seam at the base of the neck.

## BASIC SEWING SKILLS

If you are sewing your Fleecie Pet by machine, you will need to use a medium length running stitch to sew your Fleecie Pet together and stitch the clothes. The fleece clothes also have a small zigzag stitch trim around some of the raw edges, although this is optional.

If you are sewing by hand, use a standard 'sharps' sewing needle and a small running stitch. Work a small back stitch every few stitches, for extra strength.

The Fleecie Pets' ears, feet and any patches are always worked by hand using a standard 'sharps' sewing needle. You also need to close the gap used for stuffing.

### Embroidering eyes, nose and mouth

The Fleecie Pets' features are embroidered after the animal has been stuffed and shaped. The features are embroidered with three strands of embroidery thread, using the same colour throughout. This will be either black, dark grey or dark brown, depending on the animal you are making.

*Satin stitch*

Most of the Fleecie Pets' noses are worked in a basic straight satin stitch. This is a series of running stitches worked closely together so that the area is completely covered. Remember to take care to keep the stitches smooth and the tension even (see above).

Some of the Fleecie Pets' nostrils are marked by a stitch called a 'French knot'. To make a French knot, bring your needle out in the position where you want the

*French knot*                    *Back stitch*

knot. Wind your thread twice round the needle as shown in the diagram, keeping the needle as close as you can to the fabric. Insert the point of the needle back through the fabric, just by your starting point. Now gently push the threads down the needle and pull your thread through (see above).

The Fleecie Pets' mouths are worked in simple back stitch – each back stitch should be about 3 or 4 mm (1/8 in) long (see above right).

## Stuffing your Fleecie Pet and closing the gap

Always use a small amount of toy filling at a time when you are stuffing your Fleecie Pet. Also, try not to push each bit in too hard or your Fleecie Pet will look lumpy. You will need to stuff your Fleecie Pet's head firmly. This will allow you to ease the face into shape as you go. The body and limbs should be stuffed less firmly so that your Fleecie Pet has a nice squashy feel. You will probably find it easiest to stuff the head first, then the legs and arms and finally the torso. You can push the stuffing into the Fleecie Pet using the blunt end of a pencil or something similar – but make sure you don't use anything too sharp or push too hard or you may break the stitching.

When you are satisfied with the look of your Fleecie Pet, sew up the gap using slip stitch. Following the line of the seam, pick up a tiny amount of fabric on one side with your needle. Then pick up a tiny amount on the opposite side, about 3 mm (1/8 in) further along. Work a few stitches like this at a time before pulling your thread taut. Continue in this way until the gap is fully closed (see page 13, top left).

## BASIC KNITTING SKILLS

For knitting the Fleecie Pet jumpers and accessories, you will need to know some simple knitting techniques, such as how to cast on and cast (bind) off, and work knit and purl stitches. You will also need to know how to increase and decrease the number of stitches on your needle (see Knitting abbreviations, page 13).

You will also need to know how to piece the knitted garments together and conceal any loose ends neatly. Because the garments are small, the best method to use is called 'weaving', or 'mattress stitch'. Using a tapestry needle and the wool you have used for knitting the garment, join the side seams by inserting the needle on the reverse side under the horizontal loop by the edge stitch of one piece then under the corresponding horizontal loop in the second piece (see page 13, top right). For shoulder seams, the pieces are joined in a similar way, taking the needle under the knitted stitch of one piece then under the corresponding knitted stitch of the second piece.

If you want to find out more information about knitting techniques, there are many books available on the subject and several internet sites where you can pick up the information for free.

## A word on tension

The tension (sometimes called 'gauge') of a piece of knitting is a way of expressing how many stitches and rows there are in a particular sized square of the work. Getting the tension right means that the finished item will be the right size. All the garments and accessories in this book have a fairly taut look to them because this looks better on items that are so small.

*Closing the gap*

*Joining knitted pieces*

To make sure your tension is correct, you should knit a tension square. Using size 3.75 mm (US 5) needles and double knitting yarn, cast on 10 stitches. Work 12 rows in stocking (stockinette) stitch, then cast off. Your finished square should measure 4 x 4 cm (1½ x 1½ in). If your tension is noticeably tighter or looser, try using needles that are 0.25 mm (a single size) larger or smaller.

## Knitting abbreviations

The following knitting abbreviations are used in the knitting instructions for the Fleecie Pets' clothes and accessories.

**alt** = alternative – as in every alt row

**beg** = beginning

**k** = knit (This is the basic knitting stitch and is sometimes also called 'plain' knitting. The knitted fabric created by working rows of knit stitches is called 'garter' stitch. A few rows of garter stitch are worked at the bottom edges of the jumper and sleeves to give the garments a firmer edging. Garter stitch is also used for some of the accessories.)

**p** = purl

**st st** = stocking (stockinette) stitch (This is the name given to knitted fabric that has been created by knitting one row then purling one row. It is the main stitch used for the Fleecie Pet jumpers and some of the accessories. The right side of the fabric is the 'knit' side.)

**st(s)** = stitch (stitches)

**tog** = together – as in k2tog or p2tog (Sometimes you will need to knit or purl two stitches together in order to decrease the width of your work. Knitting 2 stitches together results in a stitch that slants to the right.)

**ssk** = slip 1, slip 1, K1 (This is another way of decreasing and results in a stitch that slants to the left and is a mirror image of knitting 2 stitches together. Start by slipping 1 stitch and the next stitch separately onto your needle as if you were beginning to knit them. Then, using the left-hand needle, knit through the front loops of the two stitches together.)

**m1** = make one stitch (Sometimes you will need to make a stitch by picking up the strand of wool lying between the stitch just worked and the next stitch and working into the back of it.)

**inc** = increase – as in inc1 stitch (Sometimes you will need to increase the number of stitches on your needle by knitting or purling into a stitch as normal, but keeping the stitch on your needle instead of slipping it off then knitting or purling again into the back of the stitch.)

## BASIC CROCHET SKILLS

The only crochet you will need to know is how to make a chain. This stitch is used only for the handle and button loop of Spangles the Cat's handbag (see page 55) and for the ties at the neck of the cape in the Fleecie Pet Accessories chapter (see page 76).

To start a chain from the end of a piece of knitting, insert your hook through the last knitting stitch. Draw the 'tail' of wool round the hook and use the hook to pull it through the loop. Pull fairly firmly. Repeat this simple process for the required number of chains or until your chain reaches the required length, taking care to keep your chains an equal size. When you have finished, simply pull the strand completely through the final loop. To make a chain beginning with a loose strand of wool, start by making a slipstitch on your crochet hook, in the same way as you would for casting on knitting (see below).

## A NOTE ON MEASUREMENTS

All the measurements in the book are given in metric units (millimetres or centimetres) with the measurement in inches and fractions of an inch given in brackets afterwards. It is difficult to convert small measurements exactly so figures have been rounded up or down, usually to the nearest $1/4$ in. In some cases, the measurement is given as 'between $1/4$ in and $1/2$ in'. Because the conversions are not exact, it is important that you follow one system only rather than mix the two.

*Making a crochet chain*

*Make a loop with your wool and push your crochet hook through the loop.*

*Pull gently on the yarn ends to tighten. This will form your first loop.*

*To hold your work firmly, loop the yarn around your little finger, take it across your palm and behind your index finger.*

*Holding the base of your first loop with your thumb and middle finger to keep it steady, pass your hook under the yarn.*

*Use the hook to pull the yarn through the loop already formed and let your first loop drop.*

*Continue making stitches in this way to form a chain.*

# Starting a Fleecie Pet

Nearly every Fleecie Pet is started in the same way, before you go on to give each one its unique features and clothes. Follow these 5 simple steps for each Pet and then turn to the individual project pages for the final instructions.

Check each Pet's list of materials to see what kind of fleece and templates are required before you begin.

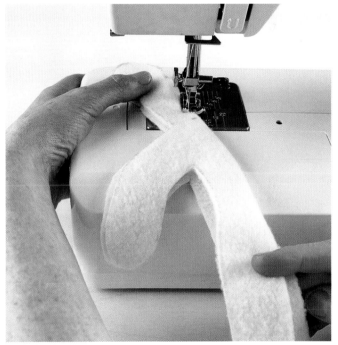

1 Photocopy or trace the body template on page 85 and the appropriate head template (see pages 84–94) and cut them out. Tape the head to the body, (see page 11). Place one of the pieces of fleece face down on a hard, flat surface. Pin the template onto the fleece or hold it firmly in place and trace around it using the water-soluble pen or quilter's pencil. Make sure that any obvious pile runs down the length of the Pet shape, from the ears to the tips of the toes. Mark the position for the body dart with the water-soluble pen. Now cut out the shape. Remember, you only need to cut out one shape at this stage. This is called the Pet shape.

2 Fold the shape in half lengthways, so that the fleecy side (the right side) of the fabric is on the inside. Sew the body dart – from the tip of the nose into the neck, then from the neck outwards to the tummy – using a small running stitch or medium length machine stitch.

3 Lay the Pet shape down on the second rectangle of fleece so that the fleecy sides (the right sides) of both pieces are facing. Make sure that any obvious pile runs down the length of the second piece of fabric, in the same direction as the fleece on the Pet shape. Secure the two pieces of fabric together with pins and, if preferred, baste the pieces together with large running stitches. Then machine stitch or sew round the Pet shape, 4 mm (1/4 in) from the outside edge, leaving an opening at one side for stuffing, as shown on the template.

If you are sewing by machine, you will get the best results if you sew from the left side of the waist to the crotch first, then from the right side of the waist to the crotch. Then rejoin your thread at the left side of the waist and complete. This will avoid any tendency for the fabric to slip and will ensure you get professional looking results.

4 Trim away excess fabric on the second piece of fleece to match the Pet shape, taking care not to cut through the stitching. Make a snip in the seam allowance at the Pet's crotch, taking care not to cut into the stitching. This will prevent any puckering round the crotch on the finished toy.

5 Turn the Pet right side out through the gap in its side. Now stuff the Pet with the polyester toy filling. Stuff the head firmly, easing the face into shape as you go and remembering not to stuff the ears. Stuff the body and limbs less firmly so the finished Fleecie Pet will have a nice squashy feel. Then sew up the gap using slip stitch.

The following Fleecie Pets will need an additional step to add patches or to shape the face, during these initial steps.

## Patches the Dog

**After step 2:** Position the leg patch on the pattern piece, about half way down one leg, making sure that the straight edge of the patch lines up with the outer raw edge of the leg. Oversew the patch onto the leg using small stitches which should be virtually invisible on the finished patch. (The eye patch is sewn on after the dog has been stuffed.) See page 84 for patch template.

## Squealy the Piglet

**After step 2:** Cut out a small oval snout and place, fleece side up, on the face. It should be in the centre of the face with the top edge of the snout 2.5 cm (1 in) below the top raw edge of the head. Baste the snout in position and sew round it, very close to the outside edge, using a small back stitch or short machine stitch.

## Joe the Monkey

**After step 2:** Place the face template (see page 90) on the reverse of the beige fleece, making sure that any pile runs down the length of the face, and pin it to hold it down. Draw round it using the water-soluble pen and cut it out. Position the face on the head so that the lower edge of the face is in line with the neck and baste in place with large running stitches. Machine stitch round the entire face, close to the edge, or oversew using matching thread and small stitches which should be virtually invisible.

## Spangles the Cat

**After step 1:** Cut out the patches from the white fleece and position the patches as shown on the template (see page 88), making sure that the outer edge of the patches line up with the outer raw edge of the face. Oversew the patches onto the face with white thread, using small stitches which should be virtually invisible.

# Patches the Dog

With his laid-back attitude and smart nautical stripes, Patches likes nothing better than messing around in boats – but always wears his armbands just in case. In a soft shade of milky coffee with splashes of dark cocoa, Patches will make a loyal and faithful companion for any dog lover and won't ever need taking for a walk.

## MATERIALS

### For the dog

- 2 pieces of pale brown fleece, each measuring 22 x 34 cm (9 x 13 in) (if the fleece has an obvious pile, this should run down the longer length of the fabric)
- Small scrap of dark brown fleece for the patches
- Matching threads for both fleece colours
- 15–20 g ($^1/_2$–$^3/_4$ oz) polyester toy filling
- Black embroidery thread

### For the swimsuit and armbands

- Piece of striped navy/white cotton jersey, approximately 15 x 22 cm (6 x 9 in) (the stripes should run across the longer length of the fabric)
- 2 rectangles of orange polyester or nylon fabric (such as that used for lightweight raincoats), each measuring 7 x 11 cm (3 x 4$^1/_2$ in)
- Small amount of polyester toy filling
- Matching threads for both fabrics

## TOOLS

- Access to a photocopier or a sheet of tracing paper and pencil
- Scissors
- Sticky tape
- Dressmakers' pins
- Water-soluble pen or quilter's pencil
- Sewing machine (optional)
- Sewing needle
- Embroidery needle

## TO MAKE THE DOG

To begin the Dog, see *Starting a Fleecie Pet* (pages 15–17) for full instructions.

1 Shape the dog's ears by folding them down and securing them in place by working a few small stitches on the underside of the ears, close to the tip. These stitches will be invisible on the finished Fleecie Pet.

2 To shape the dog's feet, turn up 4 cm (1½ in) at the end of each leg and hold in place so that the foot is at a right angle to the leg. Now, using the thread double for extra strength and starting at one of the side seams, work several large, loose slip stitches across the curve at the front of the ankle. To make sure that the finished foot is at a right angle to the leg, the slip stitches will need to pick up fabric 7 or 8 mm (¼ in) either side of the front ankle crease. Pull up the thread fairly tightly and secure.

3 Cut out the eye patch (see page 84 for template) from the dark brown fleece. Position the patch using the photograph as a guide, and oversew in place. Mark the position of the dog's eyes, nose and mouth with the water-soluble pen, again using the photograph as a guide. With three strands of black embroidery thread, stitch the eyes by working several 7-mm (¼-in) vertical stitches in and out of the same holes. For the nose, work a small upside down triangle in satin stitch. Add the mouth using back stitch.

4 To mark the dog's fingers and toes, use three strands of black embroidery thread. Secure the thread invisibly in the side seam and take the needle out at the starting point for the base of the first finger or toe. Now take the thread over the end of the paw, through the back, and then out through the front, ready to form the next finger or toe. Pull the thread fairly tightly so that it stays in position. Work two more fingers or toes in the same way. Finally, secure the thread invisibly in the side seam of the paw.

## TO MAKE THE SWIMSUIT & ARMBANDS

### For the swimsuit

1 Photocopy or trace the swimsuit template on page 84 and cut it out. Place the swimsuit template on the cotton jersey, making sure that the stripes run across the width of the swimsuit, and cut out two pieces. Mark the position of the small dots along both sides with the water-soluble pen. Sew the shoulders of the swimsuit, allowing a 5-mm (¼-in) seam allowance. Then sew the crotch seam and the side seams up to the small dots.

2 Roll over the raw edge around the neck hole and slip stitch in place on the inside. Do the same around the armholes and leg openings.

### For the armbands

1 Fold the orange fabric in half widthways with right sides facing, so that the two short sides meet. Seam along the shorter side, 5 mm (¼ in) from the outside edge.

2 Turn under 5 mm (¼ in) of both raw edges and press in place firmly using your fingers or nails to mark the crease. Bring the raw edges together so that you have a shape a bit like a ring jelly mould, with the right side of the fabric on the outside. Stuff lightly with filling and slip stitch the raw edges together. You may find it easier to slip stitch part of the way round before stuffing. Work a line of small running stitch round the middle of each armband.

# Sniffy the Mouse

Everyone knows that white mice make great pets and Sniffy is no exception. Her eyes are worked slightly smaller and closer together than most Fleecie Pets' to give them a cute 'beady' look. Her flowery skirt and heart motif sweater combine to give her a contemporary country feel. Best of all, she won't ever frighten a living soul.

## MATERIALS

### For the mouse
- 2 pieces of white fleece, each measuring 22 x 34 cm (9 x 13 in) (if the fleece has an obvious pile, this should run down the longer length of the fabric)
- Matching thread
- 15–20 g ($^1/_2$–$^3/_4$ oz) polyester toy filling
- Black embroidery thread

### For the clothes
- Small amount (approximately 15 g/$^1/_2$ oz) of lime green double knitting wool for the sweater
- Oddment of bright pink double knitting wool for the sweater heart motif
- Piece of printed floral cotton or cotton mix fabric for the skirt, measuring 13 x 30 cm (5$^1/_4$ x 12 in) (if your fabric has an obvious direction, the pattern should run down the shorter length of the fabric)
- Matching thread
- 17 cm (7 in) white elastic cord for the waistband of the skirt

## TOOLS
- Access to a photocopier or a sheet of tracing paper and pencil
- Scissors
- Sticky tape
- Dressmakers' pins
- Water-soluble pen or quilter's pencil
- Sewing machine (optional)
- Sewing needle
- Embroidery needle
- Pair of size 3.75 mm (US 5) knitting needles
- 4 row markers or small safety pins for knitting
- Tapestry needle
- Small safety pin for threading the elastic cord
- Iron

## TO MAKE THE MOUSE

To begin the Mouse, see *Starting a Fleecie Pet* (pages 15–17) for full instructions.

1 Shape the mouse's ears by pinching the base of each ear so that the outer edges are brought forwards to form a small pleat. Using the thread double for extra strength, secure the pleat by hand stitching through the base of the ear from the outer side to the inner side and back again. Pull the thread firmly before securing it invisibly in the side seam and trim closely.

2 To shape the feet, turn up 5 cm (2 in) at the end of each leg and hold in place so that the foot is at a right angle to the leg. Now, using the thread double for extra strength and starting at one of the side seams, work several large, loose slip stitches across the curve at the front of the ankle. To make sure that the finished foot is at a right angle to the leg, the slip stitches will need to pick up fabric 7 or 8 mm (1/4 in) either side of the front ankle crease. Pull up the thread fairly tightly and secure.

3 Mark the position of the eyes, nose and mouth with the water-soluble pen, using the photograph as a guide. The eyes should be about 1.25 cm (1/2 in) apart. With three strands of black embroidery thread, stitch the eyes by working several 5-mm (1/4-in) vertical stitches in and out of the same holes. For the nose, work a small horizontal rectangle in satin stitch. Add the mouth using back stitch. With a single strand of embroidery thread, sew three whiskers on each cheek.

4 To mark the fingers and toes, use three strands of black embroidery thread. Secure the thread invisibly in the side seam and take the needle out at the starting point for the base of the first finger or toe. Now take the thread over the end of the paw, through the back, and then out through the front, ready to form the next finger or toe. Pull the thread fairly tightly so that it stays in position. Work two more fingers or toes in the same way. Finally, secure the thread invisibly in the side seam of the paw.

## TO MAKE THE SWEATER AND SKIRT
### For the sweater

**Abbreviations:** see page 13.

**Tension:** 10 sts and 12 rows to 4 cm (1½ in) square in st st. If your tension is noticeably tighter or looser, try using needles that are 0.25 mm larger or smaller.

**Note:** When working the heart motif, twist the green and pink yarns round each other when you are changing colour, on the wrong side of the work, to avoid any holes.

### Front
Cast on 19 stitches in green. K 4 rows. Beg with a k row, work 4 rows in st st.

**Next row** k 9. Join pink yarn and k1. Pick up green yarn and k to end.

**Next row** p 8 green, p 3 pink, p green to end.

**Next row** k 8 green, k 3 pink, k green to end. Mark beg and end of this row with a row marker or small safety pin (this will be your guide to sewing on the sleeves).

**Next row** p 7 green, p 5 pink, p green to end.

**Next row** k 7 green, k 5 pink, k green to end.

**Next row** p 6 green, p 7 pink, p green to end.

**Next row** k 6 green, k 7 pink, k green to end.

**Next row** p 6 green, p 7 pink, p green to end.

**Next row** k 6 green, k 3 pink, k 1 green, k 3 pink, k green to end.

**Next row** p 7 green, p 1 pink, p 3 green, p 1 pink, p green to end.

Continue in st st in green only for another 4 rows, ending with a p row.

To shape shoulders, cast off 4 sts at beg of next 2 rows. Continue in st st on remaining 11 sts and work 6 rows, ending with a p row.

Cast off loosely.

### Back
Work as for front, but omitting heart motif. Mark each end of 7th row of st st with a row marker or small safety pin.

### Sleeves (make 2)
Cast on 19 stitches. K 4 rows. Beg with a k row, work 12 rows in st st. Cast off loosely.

### To make up
Using the tapestry needle, join shoulder seams and side seams of neck. Sew top edge of sleeves to jumper, between row markers. Now stitch sleeve and side seams. For more information on making up, see page 12.

> **Tip** If you leave long tails of wool when you cast on and off – 15-20 cm (6-8 in) is ideal, you will have plenty of wool to sew the jumper together, and will save yourself time sewing in loose ends.

# For the skirt

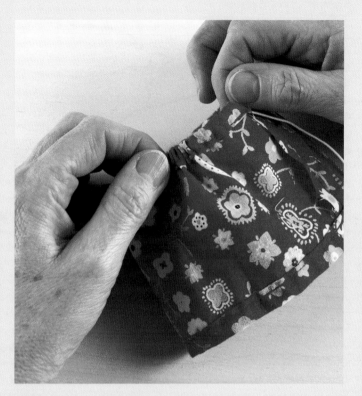

**1** Fold the piece of printed floral cotton in half widthways, with right sides facing, so that the two short sides meet. Now sew the back seam of the skirt, allowing a 5-mm (¹/₄-in) seam allowance. Press the seam open with the iron. Turn up 5 mm (¹/₄ in) at the raw edge of the skirt hem. Press in place. Turn up another 5 mm (¹/₄ in) and press again. Stitch close to the folded edge – use a machine running stitch if sewing by machine or a small hemming (slip) stitch if sewing by hand.

**2** To make the waistband, turn down 5 mm (¹/₄ in) at the top raw edge and press in place. Turn down another 5 mm (¹/₄ in) and press again. Stitch as close as possible to the folded edge, leaving a 1-cm (³/₈-in) gap at the back of the skirt for threading the elastic cord. Using the small safety pin, thread the elastic cord through the waistband casing. Knot the ends of the elastic together tightly and trim.

**Idea** *To make a country-style brother for Sniffy, make another mouse and dress him in checked trousers (see page 45 for trouser instructions) rather than a floral skirt. An outfit in shades of red and mid-blue would be perfect.*

# Squealy the Piglet

Made in the softest pale pink fleece, Squealy has no interest whatever in wallowing in the mud and getting grubby. And unlike some of her sty mates, she believes in watching her weight so she can show off her new bikini. Squealy's eyes are more widely spaced and higher up than most Fleecie Pets which give them an endearing piggy look that will delight any fan of these intelligent farmyard favourites.

## MATERIALS

### For the piglet

- 2 pieces of pale pink fleece, each measuring 22 x 34 cm (9 x 13 in) (if the fleece has an obvious pile, this should run down the longer length of the fabric)
- Matching thread
- 15–20 g ($^1/_2$–$^3/_4$ oz) polyester toy filling
- Dark grey embroidery thread

### For the bikini

- Piece of printed cotton or cotton mix fabric, measuring 15 x 30 cm (6 x 12 in) (a small print like the patchwork fabric used here is ideal)
- 2 x 15-cm (6-in) lengths of narrow ribbon for the bikini straps
- Small amount of contrasting ribbon for the bow on the bikini top (or a small readymade bow)
- 17 cm (7 in) white elastic cord for the waistband of the bikini shorts
- Matching thread

## TOOLS

- Access to a photocopier or a sheet of tracing paper and pencil
- Scissors
- Sticky tape
- Dressmakers' pins
- Water-soluble pen or quilter's pencil
- Sewing machine (optional)
- Sewing needle
- Embroidery needle
- Small safety pin for threading the elastic cord
- Iron

## TO MAKE THE PIGLET

To begin the Piglet, see *Starting a Fleecie Pet* (pages 15–17) for full instructions.

1   Shape the piglet's ears by folding them down and pulling them slightly outwards, away from the face. Secure the ears in place by working a few small stitches on the underside of each ear, close to the tip. These stitches will be invisible on the finished Fleecie Pet.

2   To shape the trotters, turn up 3 cm (1¼ in) at the end of each leg and hold in place so that the foot is at a right angle to the leg. Now, using the thread double for strength and starting at one of the side seams, work several large, loose slip stitches across the curve at the front of the ankle. To make sure that the finished trotter is at a right angle to the leg, the slip stitches will need to pick up fabric 7 or 8 mm (¼ in) either side of the front ankle crease. Pull up the thread fairly tightly and secure.

3   Mark the position of the eyes, nose and mouth with the water-soluble pen, using the photograph as a guide. The eyes should be just below the ears and about 2.5 cm (1 in) apart. With three strands of dark grey embroidery thread, stitch the eyes by working several 8-mm (¼-in) vertical stitches in and out of the same holes. For the nose, work a few tiny vertical stitches in and out of the same holes – or you may prefer to use a French knot (see page 11). Add the mouth using back stitch.

4   To mark the piglet's toes, use three strands of dark grey embroidery thread. Secure the thread invisibly in the side seam and take the needle out at the centre of each trotter, about 8 mm (¼ in) in from the tip. Now take the thread over the end of the trotter, through the back, and out through the side seam where you can secure the thread invisibly.

## TO MAKE THE BIKINI TOP AND SHORTS
### For the bikini top

1 Photocopy or trace the bikini top template on page 86 and cut it out. Cut out two identical bikini top pieces from the cotton or cotton-mix print fabric. One piece will be the front and the other will be the lining. Pin or baste the two pieces with right sides facing and sew along the top edge, 5 mm (¹⁄₄ in) from the outside edge.

2 Open the bikini top out from the bottom edge and, with right sides facing, sew the back seam of the bikini top and lining, again allowing a 5-mm (¹⁄₄-in) seam allowance.

3 Trim the tip off the top of the bikini 'cups' close to the seam and turn the bikini top right side out. Tie a tight knot at one end of each piece of the bikini strap ribbon and, from the inside, thread through the top of each bikini cup. Turn up 5 mm (¹⁄₄ in) along the raw edges and slip stitch the bikini top and lining together. Make the small bow and stitch it to the centre of the bikini top.

Tip If making the bikini top looks a bit fiddly, you could make a quick halter neck alternative with ribbon. Simply seam down the shorter length of a 12.5-cm (5-in) piece of 5-cm (2-in) wide ribbon. Fold the circle of ribbon in half so the raw edges of the seam are on the inside and slip stitch the long edges together. To finish, tie a single length of narrow ribbon round the centre of the bikini top to form two equal length straps.

## For the bikini shorts

1 Photocopy or trace the bikini shorts template on page 86 and cut it out. Cut out two pieces of cotton or cotton mix fabric for the bikini shorts. With right sides of the fabric facing, stitch the crotch seams, allowing a 5-mm (¹/₄-in) seam allowance. Press the seams open with the iron.

2 Keeping the right sides of the fabric facing, match front and back crotch seams then stitch inside leg seams, again allowing a 5-mm (¹/₄-in) seam allowance. Press seams open. Turn up 5 mm (¹/₄ in) at the raw edge of each leg hem and press in place. Turn up another 5 mm (¹/₄ in) and press again. Stitch close to the folded edge using a machine running stitch if sewing by machine, or a small hemming (slip) stitch if sewing by hand.

3 To make the waistband, turn down 5 mm (¹/₄ in) at the top raw edge and press in place. Turn down another 5 mm (¹/₄ in) and press again. Stitch as close as possible to the folded edge, leaving a 1-cm (³/₈-in) gap at the back of the shorts for threading the elastic cord. Using the small safety pin, thread the elastic cord through the waistband casing. Knot the ends of the elastic together tightly and trim.

# Bruce the Koala

Bruce is rather more energetic than the average koala and wants a more interesting life than hanging about in trees, munching eucalyptus leaves. With his colourful shorts and zany top, he's ready to spend his day surfing the ocean waves and posing on the beach. He would make a perfect companion for girl koalas and koala lovers the world over.

## MATERIALS

**For the koala**
- 2 pieces of brown-grey fleece, each measuring 22 x 34 cm (9 x 13 in) (if the fleece has an obvious pile, this should run down the longer length of the fabric)
- Matching thread
- 15–20 g ($^1/_2$–$^3/_4$ oz) polyester toy filling
- Black embroidery thread

**For the clothes**
- Piece of orange fleece for the vest, measuring 12 x 20 cm (4$^3/_4$ x 8 in) (if the fleece has an obvious pile, this should run down the shorter length of the fabric)
- Scrap of turquoise fleece for the fish motif
- Piece of printed floral cotton or cotton mix fabric for the shorts, measuring 14 x 28 cm (5$^1/_2$ x 11 in) (if your fabric has an obvious direction, the pattern should run down the shorter length of the fabric)
- Matching threads
- Tiny button for the fish eye
- 17 cm (7 in) white elastic cord for the waistband of the shorts

## TOOLS

- Access to a photocopier or a sheet of tracing paper
- Pencil
- Scissors
- Sticky tape
- Dressmakers' pins
- Water-soluble pen or quilter's pencil
- Sewing machine (optional)
- Sewing needle
- Embroidery needle
- Small safety pin for threading the elastic cord
- Iron

## TO MAKE THE KOALA

To begin the Koala, see *Starting a Fleecie Pet* (pages 15–17) for full instructions.

1 Shape the koala's ears by running a small line of running stitch across the base of the ear on the front side, using the thread double for extra strength. Pull the thread so the fabric is slightly gathered before securing it invisibly in the side seam, then trim closely.

2 To shape the feet, turn up 3.5 cm (1½ in) at the end of each leg and hold in place so that the foot is at a right angle to the leg. Now, using the thread double for strength and starting at one of the side seams, work several large, loose slip stitches across the curve at the front of the ankle. To make sure that the finished foot is at a right angle to the leg, the slip stitches will need to pick up fabric 7 or 8 mm (¼ in) either side of the front ankle crease. Pull up the thread fairly tightly and secure.

3 Mark the position of the koala's eyes, nose and mouth with the water-soluble pen, using the photograph as a guide. The eyes should be about 2 cm (¾ in) apart. With three strands of black embroidery thread, stitch the eyes by working several 5-mm (¼-in) vertical stitches in and out of the same holes. For the nose, work a vertical rectangle in satin stitch. Add the mouth using back stitch.

4 To mark the fingers and toes, use three strands of black embroidery thread. Secure the thread invisibly in the side seam and take the needle out at the starting point for the base of the first finger or toe. Now take the thread over the end of the paw, through the back, and then out through the front, ready to form the next finger or toe. Pull the thread fairly tightly so that it stays in position. Work two more fingers or toes in the same way. Secure the thread invisibly in the side seam of the paw.

## TO MAKE THE SHORTS AND VEST

### For the shorts

1 Photocopy or trace the shorts template on page 87 and cut it out. Cut out two pieces of patterned fabric for the shorts.

2 With right sides of the fabric facing, stitch the crotch seams, allowing a 5-mm (¹/₄-in) seam allowance. Press the seams open with the iron. Keeping the right sides of the fabric facing, match front and back crotch seams then stitch inside leg seams, again allowing a 5-mm (¹/₄-in) seam allowance. Press seams open.

3 To make the waistband, turn down 5 mm (¹/₄ in) at the top raw edge and press in place. Turn down another 5 mm (¹/₄ in) and press again. Stitch as close as possible to the folded edge, leaving a 1-cm (³/₈-in) gap at the back of the shorts for threading the elastic cord. Using the small safety pin, thread the elastic cord through the waistband casing. Knot the ends of the elastic together tightly and trim. Turn up 5 mm (¹/₄ in) at the raw edge of each leg hem and press in place. Turn up another 5 mm (¹/₄ in) and press again. Stitch close to the folded edge using a machine running stitch if sewing by machine, or a small hemming (slip) stitch if sewing by hand.

## For the vest

**OPTIONAL EXTRA**

If you are using a sewing machine to make Bruce's clothes, machine round the finished neck opening using a small zigzag stitch. Do the same round the bottom of the vest. This gives a really nice finish but it's not essential.

1 Photocopy or trace the vest template on page 87 and cut it out. Cut out two vest front/back pieces from the orange fleece, making sure that any obvious pile runs down the length of the vest. To prepare the fish appliqué, trace the fish shape onto the backing paper of a small piece of bonding web using an ordinary pencil. Next, with the iron on a warm setting, iron the bonding web onto the reverse side of the turquoise fleece. Cut the fish out carefully. Peel off the backing paper and position the appliqué on the front of the vest as shown on the template. Iron the appliqué in place – you may find it easier to do this by ironing the top on the reverse. Machine or hand stitch round the fish. Sew on the tiny button for the fish's eye.

2 Sew shoulder and side seams of the vest, allowing a 5-mm (¹/₄-in) seam allowance. Trim shoulder seam to about 1 mm (¹/₁₆ in) from stitching (this will help make the finished vest look neater). Now turn the vest the right way out.

**Tip** If making an appliqué seems too fiddly, take a look in your local haberdashery or craft stores for ready-made appliqués or fish shaped buttons.

# Snowy the Polar Bear Cub

This little polar bear cub is sweet and icy cool. Her pristine pink frock looks a treat on her soft white fur and her favourite pastime is posing and looking pretty while the other animals get on with the work. She would be a great choice of Fleecie Pet for any little girl who loves teddy bears and all things pink.

## MATERIALS

**For the bear**

- 2 pieces of white fleece, each measuring 22 x 34 cm (9 x 13 in) (if the fleece has an obvious pile, this should run down the longer length of the fabric)
- Matching thread
- 15–20 g ($^1/_2$–$^3/_4$ oz) polyester toy filling
- Dark grey embroidery thread

**For the clothes**

- A piece of bright pink fleece fabric, measuring 16 x 26 cm ($6^1/_4$ x $10^1/_4$ in) (if the fleece has an obvious pile, this should run down the shorter length of the fabric)
- Small piece of pale pink fleece for appliqué
- Small piece of bonding web
- Matching threads

## TOOLS

- Access to a photocopier or a sheet of tracing paper
- Pencil
- Scissors
- Sticky tape
- Dressmakers' pins
- Water-soluble pen or quilter's pencil
- Sewing machine (optional)
- Sewing needle
- Embroidery needle
- Iron

## TO MAKE THE POLAR BEAR CUB

To begin the Polar Bear cub, see *Starting a Fleecie Pet* (pages 15–17) for full instructions.

1 To define the ears, work a stitch that looks like an upside down 'V'. Using the thread double, secure it invisibly in the side seam just by the ear. Take the needle out through the base of the front of the ear, about 2 mm ($^1/_{12}$ in) from the outer edge. Then take the needle down through the fabric at the centre, just near the tip of the ear. Pick up a tiny amount of fabric at the back of the ear before taking your needle out to the front again in almost the same place. Take the thread through the lower part of the ear, just in from the inside edge. Pull the thread quite tightly to give the ears a slight curve and secure.

2 To shape the bear cub's feet, turn up 3 cm (1$^1/_4$ in) at the end of each leg and hold in place so that the foot is at a right angle to the leg. Now, using the thread double for extra strength and starting at one of the side seams, work several large, loose slip stitches across the curve at the front of the ankle. To make sure that the finished foot is at a right angle to the leg, the slip stitches will need to pick up fabric 7 or 8 mm ($^1/_4$ in) either side of the front ankle crease. Pull up the thread fairly tightly and secure.

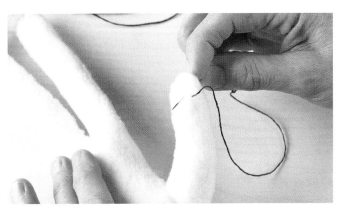

3 Mark the position of the bear cub's eyes, nose and mouth with the water-soluble pen, using the photograph as a guide. The eyes should be about 2 cm ($^3/_4$ in) apart. With three strands of dark grey embroidery thread, stitch the eyes by working several 5-mm ($^1/_4$-in) vertical stitches in and out of the same holes. For the nose, work a small upside down triangle in satin stitch. Add the mouth using back stitch.

4 To mark the fingers and toes, use three strands of dark grey embroidery thread. Secure the thread invisibly in the side seam and take the needle out at the starting point for the base of the first finger or toe. Now take the thread over the end of the paw, through the back, and then out through the front, ready to form the next finger or toe. Pull the thread fairly tightly so that it stays in position. Work two more fingers or toes in the same way. Finally, secure the thread invisibly in the side seam of the paw.

# To make the dress

1 Photocopy or trace the dress template on page 88 and cut it out. Cut out two dress front/back pieces from the bright pink fleece, making sure that any obvious pile runs down the length of the dress.

**OPTIONAL EXTRA**

If you are using a sewing machine to make Snowy's clothes, machine round the finished neck opening using a small zigzag stitch. Do the same round the bottom of the tunic, stretching the material slightly as you go. This gives a really nice finish but it's not essential.

2 To prepare the heart appliqué, trace the heart shape onto the backing paper of a small piece of bonding web using an ordinary pencil. Next, with the iron on a warm setting, iron the bonding web onto the reverse side of the pale pink fleece. Cut the heart out carefully. Peel off the backing paper and position the appliqué on the front of the dress as shown on the template. Iron the appliqué in place – you may find it easier to do this by ironing the dress on the reverse. Machine or hand stitch round the heart.

3 Sew shoulder and side seams of the dress, allowing a 5-mm (1/4-in) seam allowance. Trim shoulder seam to about 1 mm (1/16 in) from stitching (this will help make the finished tunic look neater). Now turn the dress the right way out.

Tip If making an appliqué seems too fiddly, take a look in your local haberdashery or craft stores for ready-made appliqués or heart shaped buttons.

# Hoppy the Rabbit

This rabbit was the first Fleecie Pet I ever made and was inspired by the beautiful cotton Shaker and folk art rabbits from America. Hoppy is more contemporarily dressed than her ancestors but I'm sure she will be just as popular. There's something comforting about a soft rabbit and she will make a welcome addition to a nursery or young child's bedroom.

## MATERIALS

### For the rabbit

- 2 pieces of pale grey fleece, each measuring 22 x 38 cm (9 x 15 in) (if the fleece has an obvious pile, this should run down the longer length of the fabric)
- Matching thread
- 15–20 g ($^1/_2$–$^3/_4$ oz) polyester toy filling
- Black embroidery thread

### For the clothes

- Piece of yellow fleece for the tunic top, measuring 13 x 22 cm (5$^1/_4$ x 9 in) (if your fleece has an obvious pile, this should run down the shorter length of the fabric)
- A scrap of co-ordinating cotton or cotton mix fabric for the flower appliqué
- A small amount of bonding web to fasten the appliqué
- A small button for the flower centre
- Piece of striped cotton or cotton mix fabric for the trousers, measuring 20 x 30 cm (8 x 12 in) (the stripe should run down the shorter length of the fabric)
- Matching threads
- 17 cm (7 in) white elastic cord for the waistband of the trousers

## TOOLS

- Access to a photocopier or a sheet of tracing paper
- Pencil
- Scissors
- Sticky tape
- Dressmakers' pins
- Water-soluble pen or quilter's pencil
- Sewing machine (optional)
- Sewing needle
- Embroidery needle
- Small safety pin for threading the elastic cord
- Iron

## TO MAKE THE RABBIT

To begin the Rabbit, see *Starting a Fleecie Pet* (pages 15-17) for full instructions.

1 Shape the rabbit's ears by pinching the base of each ear so that the outer edges are brought forwards to form a small pleat. Using the thread double for extra strength, secure the pleat by hand stitching through the base of the ear from the outer side to the inner side and back again. Pull the thread firmly before securing it invisibly in the side seam and trim closely.

2 To shape the feet, turn up 5 cm (2 in) at the end of each leg and hold in place so that the foot is at a right angle to the leg. Now, using the thread double for extra strength and starting at one of the side seams, work several large, loose slip stitches across the curve at the front of the ankle. To make sure that the finished foot is at a right angle to the leg, the slip stitches will need to pick up fabric 7 or 8 mm ($^1/_4$ in) either side of the front ankle crease. Pull up the thread fairly tightly and secure.

3 Mark the position of the rabbit's eyes, nose and mouth with the water-soluble pen, using the photograph as a guide. The eyes should be about 2 cm ($^3/_4$ in) apart. With three strands of black embroidery thread, stitch the eyes by working several 7-mm ($^1/_4$-in) vertical stitches in and out of the same holes. For the nose, work a small upside down triangle in satin stitch. Add the mouth using back stitch.

4 To mark the fingers and toes, use three strands of black embroidery thread. Secure the thread invisibly in the side seam and take the needle out at the starting point for the base of the first finger or toe. Now take the thread over the end of the paw, through the back, and then out through the front, ready to form the next finger or toe. Pull the thread fairly tightly so that it stays in position. Work two more fingers or toes in the same way. Finally, secure the thread invisibly in the side seam of the paw.

## TO MAKE THE TUNIC TOP AND THE TROUSERS
### For the tunic top

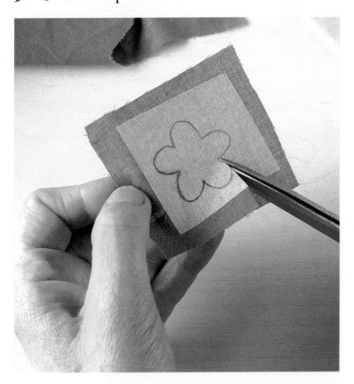

1 Photocopy or trace the tunic template on page 89 and cut it out. Cut out two tunic top front/back pieces from the yellow fleece, making sure that any obvious pile runs down the length of the top. To prepare the flower appliqué, trace the flower shape onto the backing paper of a small piece of bonding web using an ordinary pencil. Next, with the iron on a warm setting, iron the bonding web onto the reverse side of the appliqué material. Cut the flower out carefully.

2 Peel off the backing paper and position the appliqué on the front of the tunic top as indicated on the template. Iron the appliqué in place. Machine or hand stitch round the flower. Sew on the button for the flower centre.

3 Sew shoulder and side seams of the tunic top, allowing a 5-mm (¼-in) seam allowance. Trim shoulder seam to about 1 mm (¹⁄₁₆ in) from stitching (this will help make the finished tunic look neater). Now turn the tunic top the right way out.

## For the trousers

1 Photocopy or trace the trousers template on page 91 and cut it out. Cut out two pieces of striped fabric for the trousers, making sure that the stripe runs down the length of the trouser pieces. With right sides of the fabric facing, stitch the crotch seams, allowing a 5-mm (¹/₄-in) seam allowance. Press the seams open with the iron.

2 Keeping the right sides of the fabric facing, match front and back crotch seams then stitch inside leg seams, again allowing a 5-mm (¹/₄-in) seam allowance. Press seams open.

3 Turn up 5 mm (¹/₄ in) at the raw edge of each leg hem and press in place. Turn up another 5 mm (¹/₄ in) and press again. Stitch close to the folded edge using a machine running stitch if sewing by machine, or a small hemming (slip) stitch if sewing by hand. To make the waistband, turn down 5 mm (¹/₄ in) at the top raw edge and press in place. Turn down another 5 mm (¹/₄ in) and press again. Stitch as close as possible to the folded edge, leaving a 1-cm (³/₈-in) gap at the back of the trousers for threading the elastic cord. Using the small safety pin, thread the elastic cord through the waistband casing. Knot the ends of the elastic together tightly and trim.

Tip If making an appliqué seems too fiddly, take a look in your local haberdashery or craft stores for ready-made appliqués or flower shaped buttons.

# Joe the Monkey

Monkeys have been favourite toys for decades and this little primate with his cheeky grin should delight any monkey fan. His red spotty trousers give him a hint of 1950s nostalgia and his starry sweatshirt brings him bang up to date. He's more than ready to swing in the jungle or, alternatively, stand on a bedroom shelf and look appealing.

## MATERIALS

**For the monkey**
- 2 pieces of dark brown fleece, each measuring 22 x 34 cm (9 x 13 in) (if the fleece has an obvious pile, this should run down the longer length of the fabric)
- Small piece of beige fleece for the monkey's face, measuring 6 x 6 cm (2$^1/_2$ x 2$^1/_2$ in)
- Matching threads
- 15–20 g ($^1/_2$–$^3/_4$ oz) polyester toy filling
- Dark brown embroidery thread

**For the clothes**
- Piece of turquoise fleece for top, measuring 15 x 34 cm (6 x 13 in) (if the fleece has an obvious pile, this should run down the shorter length of the fabric)
- Small piece of yellow fleece for appliqué
- Small piece of bonding web
- Piece of red polka dot cotton or cotton mix fabric for the trousers, measuring 20 x 30 cm (8 x 12 in)
- Matching threads
- 17 cm (7 in) white elastic cord for the waistband of the trousers

## TOOLS
- Access to a photocopier or a sheet of tracing paper
- Pencil
- Scissors
- Sticky tape
- Dressmakers' pins
- Water-soluble pen or quilter's pencil
- Sewing machine (optional)
- Sewing needle
- Embroidery needle
- Small safety pin for threading the elastic cord
- Iron

## TO MAKE THE MONKEY

To begin the Monkey, see *Starting a Fleecie Pet* (pages 15–17) for full instructions.

1 To define the ears, work a stitch that looks like a 'V' on its side. Using the thread double, secure it invisibly in the side seam just below the ear. Take the needle out through the inside edge of the front of the ear, about 2 mm (¹/₁₂ in) from the bottom. Then take your needle down through the centre of the ear, about 2 mm (¹/₁₂ in) from the outer edge. Pick up a tiny amount of fabric at the back of the ear before taking your needle out to the front again in almost the same place. Take your thread through the upper inside edge of the ear. Pull the thread quite tightly to give the ears a slight curve and secure.

2 To shape the feet, turn up 5 cm (2 in) at the end of each leg and hold in place so that the foot is at a right angle to the leg. Now, using the thread double and starting at one of the side seams, work several large, loose slip stitches across the curve at the front of the ankle. To make sure that the finished foot is at a right angle to the leg, the slip stitches will need to pick up fabric 7 or 8 mm (¹/₄ in) either side of the front ankle crease. Pull up the thread fairly tightly and secure.

3 Mark the position of the monkey's eyes, nose and mouth with the water-soluble pen, using the photograph as a guide. The eyes should be more widely set than for most of the other Fleecie Pets – about 2.5 cm (1 in) apart is ideal. With three strands of dark brown embroidery thread, stitch the eyes by working several 8-mm (¹/₄-in) vertical stitches in and out of the same holes. For the nose, work two French knots (see page 11). Add the mouth using back stitch.

4 To mark the fingers and toes, use three strands of dark brown embroidery thread. Secure the thread invisibly in the side seam and take the needle out at the starting point about 1.5 cm (³/₄ in) from the end of the foot. Take the thread over the end of the foot, through the back, and then out through the front, ready to form the next finger or toe. Pull the thread fairly tightly so that it stays in position. Work two more fingers or toes in the same way. Finally, secure the thread invisibly in the side seam.

## TO MAKE THE SWEATSHIRT AND THE TROUSERS
### For the sweatshirt

**1** Photocopy or trace the sweatshirt templates on page 89–90 and cut them out. Cut out two sweatshirt front/back pieces and two sleeve pieces from the turquoise fleece, making sure that any obvious pile runs down the length of the top and sleeves. For the star, trace the shape onto the backing paper of a piece of bonding web using an ordinary pencil. Next, with the iron on a warm setting, iron the bonding web onto the reverse side of the piece of yellow fleece. Cut the star out carefully.

**2** Peel off the backing paper and position the appliqué on the front of the sweatshirt, as shown on the template. Iron the appliqué in place – you may find it easier to do this by ironing the top on the reverse. Machine or hand stitch round the star.

**3** Sew shoulder seams of sweatshirt allowing a 5-mm (1/4-in) seam allowance. Position sleeves between small dots, making sure that any obvious pile runs down the length of the sleeve, and stitch in place. Then sew the sleeve and side seams. Now turn the sweatshirt the right way out.

### OPTIONAL EXTRA

If you are using a sewing machine to make Joe's clothes, machine round the finished bottom of the sweatshirt using a small zigzag stitch. This gives a really nice finish but it's not essential.

## For the trousers

1 Photocopy or trace the trousers template on page 91 and cut it out. Cut out two pieces of polka dot fabric for the trousers. With right sides of the fabric facing, stitch the crotch seams, allowing a 5-mm (¹/₄-in) seam allowance. Press the seams open with the iron.

2 Keeping the right sides of the fabric facing, match front and back crotch seams then stitch inside leg seams, again allowing a 5-mm (¹/₄-in) seam allowance. Press seams open.

3 Turn up 5 mm (¹/₄ in) at the raw edge of each leg hem and press in place. Turn up another 5 mm (¹/₄ in) and press again. Stitch close to the folded edge using a machine running stitch if sewing by machine, or a small hemming (slip) stitch if sewing by hand. To make the waistband, turn down 5 mm (¹/₄ in) at the top raw edge and press in place. Turn down another 5 mm (¹/₄ in) and press again. Stitch as close as possible to the folded edge, leaving a 1-cm (³/₈-in) gap at the back of the trousers for threading the elastic cord. Using the small safety pin, thread the elastic cord through the waistband casing. Knot the ends of the elastic together tightly and trim.

Tip If making an appliqué seems too fiddly, take a look in your local haberdashery or craft stores for ready-made appliqués or star shaped buttons.

# Spangles the Cat

With her slightly haughty air, Spangles considers herself to be a step above your average family cat. She takes the utmost care of her appearance and her favourite outfit at the moment is this ballet skirt, matching jumper and girly handbag. She is a must for cat lovers everywhere and solemnly promises not to scratch the upholstery.

## MATERIALS

### For the cat
- 2 pieces of dark grey fleece, each measuring 22 x 34 cm (9 x 13 in) (if the fleece has an obvious pile, this should run down the longer length of the fabric)
- Small piece of white fleece for patches
- Matching threads
- 15–20 g ($\frac{1}{2}$–$\frac{3}{4}$ oz) polyester toy filling
- Black embroidery thread

### For the clothes
- Small amount (approximately 15 g/$\frac{1}{2}$ oz) of pale pink double knitting wool for the sweater
- Piece of pale pink polyester net fabric or tulle (similar to net but finer) for the skirt, measuring 55 x 24 cm (21$\frac{1}{2}$ x 9$\frac{1}{2}$ in)
- Piece of pale pink organza fabric for the underskirt, measuring 55 x 24 cm (21$\frac{1}{2}$ x 9$\frac{1}{2}$ in)
- Matching thread
- 2 lengths of white elastic cord, each 17-cm (7-in) long for the waistbands of the skirt and underskirt
- Small crystal button – 9 mm ($\frac{1}{4}$ in) diameter

### For the bag
- Oddment of mauve double knitting wool
- Small mother of pearl button – 9 mm ($\frac{1}{4}$ in) diameter

## TOOLS
- Access to a photocopier or a sheet of tracing paper and pencil
- Scissors
- Sticky tape
- Dressmakers' pins
- Water-soluble pen or quilter's pencil
- Sewing machine (optional)
- Sewing needle
- Embroidery needle
- Pair of size 3.75 mm (US 5) knitting needles
- A size 4 mm (US 6) crochet hook
- 4 row markers or small safety pins for knitting
- Tapestry needle
- Small safety pin for threading the elastic cord
- Iron

## TO MAKE THE CAT

To begin the Cat, see *Starting a Fleecie Pet* (pages 15–17) for full instructions.

1 To define the ears, work an upside down 'V' stitch on the front of the ear. Using the thread double, secure it invisibly in the side seam just by the ear. Take the needle out through the base of the front of the ear, about 2 mm (¹/₁₂ in) from the outer edge. Then take the needle down through the fabric at the centre of the ear, just near the tip. Pick up a tiny amount of fabric at the back of the ear before taking your needle out to the front again in almost the same place. Take your thread through the lower inside edge of the ear. Pull the thread slightly to give the ears a slight curve and secure.

2 To shape the feet, turn up 4 cm (1¹/₂ in) at the end of each leg and hold in place so that the foot is at a right angle to the leg. Now, using the thread double for extra strength and starting at one of the side seams, work several large, loose slip stitches across the curve at the front of the ankle. To make sure that the finished foot is at a right angle to the leg, the slip stitches will need to pick up fabric 7 or 8 mm (¹/₄ in) either side of the front ankle crease. Pull up the thread fairly tightly and secure.

3 Mark the position of the eyes, nose and mouth with the water-soluble pen, using the photograph as a guide. The eyes should be about 2 cm (³/₄ in) apart. With three strands of black embroidery thread, stitch the eyes by working several 5-mm (¹/₄-in) vertical stitches in and out of the same holes. For the nose, work a small upside down triangle in satin stitch. Add the mouth using back stitch. With a single strand of embroidery thread, sew three whiskers on each cheek.

4 To mark the fingers and toes, use three strands of black embroidery thread. Secure the thread invisibly in the side seam and take the needle out at the starting point for the base of the first finger or toe. Now take the thread over the end of the paw, through the back, and then out through the front, ready to form the next finger or toe. Pull the thread fairly tightly so that it stays in position. Work two more fingers or toes in the same way. Finally, secure the thread invisibly in the side seam of the paw.

## TO MAKE THE SWEATER, BAG, TUTU AND UNDERSKIRT
### For the tutu

1 Fold the piece of net fabric or tulle in half widthways, so that the two short sides meet. Now sew the back seam of the skirt, allowing a 5-mm (¼-in) seam allowance. Press the seam open with your fingers.

2 Bring the raw edges of the tutu together so that your material is double and the back seam is on the inside. To make the waistband, sew a line of stitching round the top folded edge of the skirt, about 1 cm (³/₈ in) from the edge, leaving a 1-cm (³/₈-in) gap at the back of the skirt over the seam for threading the elastic cord. Using the small safety pin, thread the elastic cord through the waistband casing. Knot the ends of the elastic together tightly and trim.

### For the underskirt

The underskirt is made in exactly the same way as the tutu except that after step 1 you will need to hem both raw edges. Turn up 5 mm (¼ in) at edges and press in place using a cool iron. Turn up another 5 mm (¼ in) at both edges and press again. Stitch close to the folded edges – use a machine running stitch if sewing by machine or a small hemming (slip) stitch if sewing by hand. Once you have done this, bring the two hemmed edges together so that the seam is on the inside and make the waistband as for the tutu, as outlined above.

# For the sweater

**Abbreviations:** see page 13.

**Tension:** 10 sts and 12 rows to 4 cm (1½ in) square in st st. If your tension is noticeably tighter or looser, try using needles that are 0.25 mm larger or smaller.

## Front
Cast on 19 stitches in pale pink. K 4 rows. Beg with a k row, work 18 rows in st st, marking the beg and end of the 7th row with a row marker or small safety pin (this will be your guide to sewing on the sleeves).
To shape shoulders, cast off 4 st at beg of next 2 rows.
Continue in st st on remaining 11 sts and work 6 rows, ending with a p row.
Cast off loosely.

## Back
Work exactly as for front.

## Sleeves (make 2)
Cast on 19 stitches. K 4 rows. Beg with a k row, work 12 rows in st st. Cast off loosely.

## To make up
Using the tapestry needle, join shoulder seams and side seams of neck. Sew top edge of sleeves to jumper, between row markers. Now stitch sleeve and side seams. For more information on making up, see page 12. Finish jumper by sewing the crystal button just below the roll neck, as shown in the main photograph.

# For the bag

**Note:** The bag is made in one piece, ending with the top flap of the bag, and is worked in garter stitch throughout.

Cast on 11 sts in mauve, leaving a 20-cm (8-in) tail which will form the bag handle.
K 2 rows.
Inc 1 st at either end of next and every alt row till there are 17 sts.
Work 13 rows.
Ssk at beg and k2tog at end of next and every alt row until there are 11 sts.
K 7 rows.
Ssk at beginning and k2tog at end of next 3 rows.
Cast off remaining 5 sts leaving a long 15-cm (6-in) 'tail' to use to make button loop.

## To make up
Fold the bottom of the bag upwards and oversew the sides of bag together using the mauve wool and tapestry needle. With 'tail' of wool at cast off edge, work 5 chain stitches using your crochet hook (see page 14 for more information). Pull end of wool through final chain and secure in place to make button loop. Make bag handle by crocheting a 5.5-cm (2¼-in) chain from the tail of wool at the cast on edge. Pull end of wool through final chain and stitch free end of handle in place. Complete the bag by sewing on the button.

**Tip** If you leave long tails of wool when you cast on and off – 15-20 cm (6-8 in) is ideal – you will have plenty of wool to sew the jumper together, and will save yourself time sewing in loose ends.

# Rumble the Bear

Cuddly bears have been around since the end of the 19th century. They are probably the most loved of all soft toys and I couldn't complete this collection without at least one. Rumble, in his cheerful red dungarees, is a hardworking, straightforward guy with respect for old-fashioned values. He will make a wonderful addition to teddy bear collections everywhere.

## MATERIALS

**For the bear**
- 2 pieces of beige fleece, each measuring 22 x 34 cm (9 x 13 in) (if the fleece has an obvious pile, this should run down the longer length of the fabric)
- Matching thread
- 15–20 g ($^1$/$_2$–$^3$/$_4$ oz) polyester toy filling
- Dark brown embroidery thread

**For the clothes**
- A piece of red needlecord fabric, measuring 25 x 30 cm (10 x 12 in) (the lines of the needlecord should run down the shorter length of the fabric)
- Matching thread
- 2 small snap fasteners
- 2 small white buttons – 9mm ($^1$/$_4$ in) diameter

## TOOLS
- Access to a photocopier or a sheet of tracing paper and pencil
- Scissors
- Sticky tape
- Dressmakers' pins
- Water-soluble pen or quilter's pencil
- Sewing machine (optional)
- Sewing needle
- Embroidery needle
- Iron

## TO MAKE THE BEAR

To begin the Bear, see *Starting a Fleecie Pet* (pages 15–17) for full instructions.

1 To define the ears, work a stitch that looks like an upside down 'V'. Using the thread double, secure it invisibly in the side seam just by the ear. Take the needle out through the base of the front of the ear, about 2 mm (1/12 in) from the outer edge. Then take the needle down through the fabric at the centre, just near the tip of the ear. Pick up a tiny amount of fabric at the back of the ear before taking your needle out to the front again in almost the same place. Take your thread through the lower part of the ear, just in from the inside edge. Pull the thread quite tightly to give the ears a slight curve and secure.

2 To shape the bear's feet, turn up 3 cm (1¼ in) at the end of each leg and hold in place so that the foot is at a right angle to the leg. Now, using the thread double for extra strength and starting at one of the side seams, work several large, loose slip stitches across the curve at the front of the ankle. To make sure that the finished foot is at a right angle to the leg, the slip stitches will need to pick up fabric 7 or 8 mm (¼ in) either side of the front ankle crease. Pull up the thread fairly tightly and secure.

3 Mark the position of the bear's eyes, nose and mouth with the water-soluble pen, using the photograph as a guide. The eyes should be about 2 cm (¾ in) apart. With three strands of dark brown embroidery thread, stitch the eyes by working several 5-mm (1/4-in) vertical stitches in and out of the same holes. For the nose, work a small upside down triangle in satin stitch. Add the mouth using back stitch.

4 To mark the fingers and toes, use three strands of dark brown embroidery thread. Secure the thread invisibly in the side seam and take the needle out at the starting point for the base of the first finger or toe. Now take the thread over the end of the paw, through the back, and then out through the front, ready to form the next finger or toe. Pull the thread fairly tightly so that it stays in position. Work two more fingers or toes in the same way. Finally, secure the thread invisibly in the side seam.

# To make the dungarees

1 Photocopy or trace the templates for the dungarees on page 93 and cut out two leg and bib pieces, two straps and one pocket. Fold in 3 mm (¹/₈ in) around pocket edges and press. Sew along the top of the pocket and stitch the pocket in place on the bib, as shown on the template. Place the two bib pieces right sides together and sew round the top and sides leaving a 5 mm (¹/₄ in) seam allowance. Turn right sides out. Sew one crotch seam on trouser pieces and press open. Pin and baste the bottom edge of the front side of the bib across the top of the crotch seam as shown and stitch 5 mm (¹/₄ in) from raw edge. Sew remaining crotch seam and inside leg seams.

2 Turn down 5 mm (¹/₄ in) round raw edge of waist and iron in place. Sew round entire waist, including bib, using a small zig zag stitch if sewing by machine or a small hemming (slip) stitch if sewing by hand. Turn up 5 mm (¹/₄ in) of the raw edge of each leg and press in place. Turn up another 5 mm (¹/₄ in) and press again. Stitch close to the folded edge using a machine running stitch if sewing by machine, or a small hemming (slip) stitch if sewing by hand.

3 For the straps, fold the long outer edges towards the middle of the strap so that they cross over slightly. Stitch along the middle of the strap using a medium zigzag stitch if sewing by machine, or a small running stitch if sewing by hand. Place the two straps at the inside back of the dungarees so that they cross and machine or hand stitch in place along the waistline, as shown. Now you can put the dungarees on your bear to measure where to put the snap fasteners on the strap fronts and reverse side of the bib before sewing on the decorative buttons.

# Scrounger the Rat

It's true that rats are not the most adored of creatures, but Scrounger is an exception.
With his patched trousers and cool bandana, he's more lovable rogue than pesky
rodent, but his piercing gaze lets you know who's boss. Scrounger will be an ideal gift for
little boys everywhere who, like this little rat, love nothing better than running round
outside and getting mucky.

## MATERIALS

**For the rat**
- 2 pieces of pale brown fleece, each measuring
  22 x 34 cm (9 x 13 in) (if the fleece has an obvious
  pile, this should run down the longer length of the
  fabric)
- Matching thread
- 15–20 g ($^1/_2$–$^3/_4$ oz) polyester toy filling
- Black embroidery thread

**For the clothes**
- Small amounts (approximately 10g/$^1/_2$ oz) of mid-
  blue and cream double knitting wool for the sweater
- Piece of pale blue chambray or light denim fabric
  for the trousers, measuring 20 x 30 cm (8 x 12 in)
- Scraps of checked red fabric for the trouser patch
  and patterned red fabric for the bandana
- Matching thread
- 17 cm (7 in) white elastic cord for the waistband of
  the trousers

## TOOLS

- Access to a photocopier or a sheet of tracing paper
  and pencil
- Scissors
- Sticky tape
- Dressmakers' pins
- Water-soluble pen or quilter's pencil
- Sewing machine (optional)
- Sewing needle
- Embroidery needle
- Pair of size 3.75 mm (US 5) knitting needles
- 4 row markers or small safety pins for knitting
- Tapestry needle
- Small safety pin for threading the elastic cord
- Iron

## TO MAKE THE RAT

To begin the Rat, see *Starting a Fleecie Pet* (pages 15–17) for full instructions.

1 Shape the rat's ears by pinching the base of each ear so that the outer edges are brought forwards to form a small pleat. Using the thread double for extra strength, secure the pleat by hand stitching through the base of the ear from the outer side to the inner side and back again. Pull the thread firmly before securing it invisibly in the side seam and trim closely.

2 To shape the feet, turn up 5 cm (2 in) at the end of each leg and hold in place so that the foot is at a right angle to the leg. Now, using the thread double for extra strength and starting at one of the side seams, work several large, loose slip stitches across the curve at the front of the ankle. To make sure that the finished foot is at a right angle to the leg, the slip stitches will need to pick up fabric 7 or 8 mm (¼ in) either side of the front ankle crease. Pull up the thread fairly tightly and secure.

3 Mark the position of the rat's eyes, nose and mouth with the water-soluble pen, using the photograph as a guide. The eyes should be about 1.5 cm (¾ in) apart. With three strands of black embroidery thread, stitch the eyes by working several 5-mm (¼-in) vertical stitches in and out of the same holes. For the nose, work a small upside down triangle in satin stitch. Add the mouth using back stitch. With a single strand of embroidery thread, sew three whiskers on each cheek.

4 To mark the fingers and toes, use three strands of black embroidery thread. Secure the thread invisibly in the side seam and take the needle out at the starting point for the base of the first finger or toe. Now take the thread over the end of the paw, through the back, and then out through the front, ready to form the next finger or toe. Pull the thread fairly tightly so that it stays in position. Work two more fingers or toes in the same way. Finally, secure the thread invisibly in the side seam of the paw.

## TO MAKE THE SWEATER, TROUSERS AND BANDANA
### For the sweater

**Abbreviations:** see page 13.

**Tension:** 10 sts and 12 rows to 4 cm (1½ in) square in st st. If your tension is noticeably tighter or looser, try using needles that are 0.25 mm larger or smaller.

**Note:** When knitting stripes, you do not need to cut the ends when you have finished each stripe. Simply leave the yarn and take it up the side of your work when you need it again, taking care not to pull it too tightly.

### Front
Cast on 19 stitches in blue. K 4 rows.
Change to cream wool and beg with a k row, work 4 rows in st st.
Rejoin blue wool and continuing in st st, work 2 rows. Continuing in st st, mark beginning and end of next row with a row marker or small safety pin (this will be your guide to sewing on the sleeves). Work one more row in st st.
Rejoin cream wool and work another 4 rows in st st.
Rejoin blue wool and work another 4 rows in st st.

Rejoin cream wool and work 2 rows in st st. Continuing in cream, shape shoulders by casting off 4 st at beg of next 2 rows.
Rejoin blue wool. Continue in st st on remaining 11 st and work 6 rows, ending with a p row.
Cast off loosely.

### Back
Work as for front.

### Sleeves (make 2)
Cast on 19 stitches in blue. K 4 rows. Change to cream wool and beg with a k row, work 4 rows in st st. Continue in st st in the blue/cream stripe pattern for another 8 rows. Cast off loosely.

### To make up
Using the tapestry needle, join shoulder seams and side seams of neck. Sew top edge of sleeves to jumper, between row markers. Now stitch sleeve and side seams. For more information on making up, see page 12.

# For the trousers

1 Photocopy or trace the trousers template on page 91 and cut it out. Scrounger's trousers should be shorter than the other Pets', so you may want to adjust the legs accordingly. Cut out two pieces of chambray or denim for the trousers. On one of the trouser pieces, sew on a 2 cm (³/₄ in) square of checked red fabric for the patch, see photo above for positioning. With right sides of the fabric facing, stitch the crotch seams, allowing a 5-mm (¹/₄-in) seam allowance. Press the seams open with the iron.

2 Keeping the right sides of the fabric facing, match front and back crotch seams then stitch inside leg seams, again allowing a 5-mm (¹/₄-in) seam allowance. Press seams open.

3 To make the waistband, turn down 5 mm (¹/₄ in) at the top raw edge and press in place. Turn down another 5 mm (¹/₄ in) and press again. Stitch as close as possible to the folded edge, leaving a 1-cm (³/₈-in) gap at the back of the trousers for threading the elastic cord. Using the small safety pin, thread the elastic cord through the waistband casing. Knot the ends of the elastic together tightly and trim. Using a needle, fray approximately 5 mm (¹/₄ in) at the lower edges of the trousers as shown.

# For the bandana

Cut out a strip of red patterned fabric measuring 2 x 17 cm (³/₄ x 7 in). Leave the raw edges unfinished and tie loosely round the neck of your finished rat.

# Fuzzy the Sheep

This groovy little sheep loves grazing and daydreaming. Her widely set eyes and curly topknot give her a distinctive look. While her funky floral trousers and sheepskin coat hark back to the dreamy days of the 1960s, Fuzzy is the epitome of 21st century cool and is looking for a like-minded owner.

## MATERIALS

### For the sheep

- 2 pieces of white fleece, each measuring 22 x 34 cm (9 x 13 in) (if the fleece has an obvious pile, this should run down the longer length of the fabric)
- Oddment of cream double knitting wool
- Matching thread
- 15–20 g (1/2–3/4 oz) polyester toy filling
- Dark brown embroidery thread

### For the clothes

- Piece of floral cotton or cotton mix fabric for the trousers, measuring 20 x 30 cm (8 x 12 in)
- Piece of sheepskin effect jacket lining or fleece for the coat, measuring 18 x 42 cm (7 x 161/2 in)
- Matching threads
- 17 cm (7 in) white elastic cord for the waistband of the trousers
- 2 small snap fasteners
- 2 small brown buttons – 9mm (1/4 in) diameter

## TOOLS

- Access to a photocopier or a sheet of tracing paper and pencil
- Scissors
- Sticky tape
- Dressmakers' pins
- Water-soluble pen or quilter's pencil
- Sewing machine (optional)
- Sewing needle
- Embroidery needle
- Pair of size 3.75 mm (US 5) knitting needles
- Small safety pin for threading the elastic cord
- Iron

## TO MAKE THE SHEEP

To begin the Sheep, see *Starting a Fleecie Pet* (pages 15–17) for full instructions.

1 Shape the sheep's ears by folding them down and pulling them slightly outwards, away from the face. Secure the ears in place by working a few small stitches on the underside of each ear. These stitches will be invisible on the finished Pet.

2 To shape the sheep's feet, turn up 3.5 cm (1¹/₂ in) at the end of each leg and hold in place so that the foot is at a right angle to the leg. Now, using the thread double for extra strength and starting at one of the side seams, work several large, loose slip stitches across the curve at the front of the ankle. To make sure that the finished foot is at a right angle to the leg, the slip stitches will need to pick up fabric 7 or 8 mm (¹/₄ in) either side of the front ankle crease. Pull up the thread fairly tightly and secure.

*Tip  To stitch the sheep's ear invisibly, first hold the ear firmly in position. Still holding the top of the ear firmly, lift the tip of the ear to reveal the underneath. Now you can make your stitches.*

3 Mark the position of the sheep's eyes, nose and mouth with the water-soluble pen, using the photograph as a guide. The eyes should be slightly higher than for most Fleecie Pets and more widely set – about 2.5 cm (1 in) apart is ideal. With three strands of dark brown embroidery thread, stitch the eyes by working a few 5-mm (¼-in) vertical stitches in and out of the same holes. Work the nose and mouth using back stitch.

4 To mark the sheep's hooves, use three strands of dark brown embroidery thread. Secure the thread invisibly in the side seam and take the needle out at the centre of each hoof, about 8 mm (¼ in) from the tip. Now take the thread over the end of the hoof, through the back, and out through the side seam where you can secure the thread invisibly.

5 To complete the sheep, make a woolly topknot. Using size 3.75 mm (US 5) knitting needles, cast on 10 stitches and knit a few rows in garter stitch. Dampen slightly and leave to dry (this will ensure the curl stays in when you unravel it). Unravel the wool and loosely wrap a length of it (approximately 40 cm/16 in) round two fingers. Slip the loops off and join at the centre to the top of the sheep's head with matching thread.

## TO MAKE THE TROUSERS AND COAT
### For the trousers

1 Photocopy or trace the trousers template on page 91 and cut it out. Cut out two pieces of floral fabric for the trousers. With right sides of the fabric facing, stitch the crotch seams, allowing a 5-mm (¹/₄-in) seam allowance. Press the seams open with the iron.

2 Keeping the right sides of the fabric facing, match front and back crotch seams then stitch inside leg seams, again allowing a 5-mm (¹/₄-in) seam allowance. Press seams open.

3 Turn up 5 mm (¹/₄ in) at the raw edge of each leg hem and press in place. Turn up another 5 mm (¹/₄ in) and press again. Stitch close to the folded edge using a machine running stitch if sewing by machine, or a small hemming (slip) stitch if sewing by hand. To make the waistband, turn down 5 mm (¹/₄ in) at the top raw edge and press in place. Turn down another 5 mm (¹/₄ in) and press again. Stitch as close as possible to the folded edge, leaving a 1-cm (³/₈-in) gap at the back of the trousers for threading the elastic cord. Using the small safety pin, thread the elastic cord through the waistband casing. Knot the ends of the elastic together tightly and trim.

## For the coat

1 Photocopy or trace the coat templates on page 91–92 and cut them out. Cut out two pockets, one back and two front pieces from the sheepskin-effect fabric. Remember that the coat has a right and left side so you will need to cut one front piece using the template the right way up and the other using the template face down. Position the pockets as shown on the template and baste in place using a few large running stitches. Because the fabric is bulky, you will probably find it easier to hand stitch rather than machine the pockets in place round the sides and base.

2 With right sides of the fabric together, sew the two fronts of the coat to the back at sleeve and side seams, allowing a 5-mm (¹/₄-in) seam. Trim the seam allowance to 1 mm (¹/₁₆ in) (this will help make the coat less bulky and give it a better fit). Turn the coat the right way out. If you are using a sewing machine to make Fuzzy's clothes, work a small zigzag stitch round the entire outer edge of the coat. This isn't essential but gives the coat a more professional finish.

3 Sew the two buttons in place on the right side of the coat, as shown in the main photograph. Overlap the right side over the left side of the coat. Sew one part of the snap fasteners on the inside of the coat, directly underneath the buttons and the corresponding parts on the top of the left side of the coat.

# Leapy the Frog

Even people who flee at the sight of a real frog would be happy to give a home to Leapy.

In his bright yellow raincoat, he's prepared for a shower or even a downpour and would

feel quite at home brightening up any bathroom. Best of all, he's not in the least bit slimy.

## MATERIALS

**For the frog**
- 2 pieces of green fleece, each measuring 22 x 34 cm (9 x 13 in) (if the fleece has an obvious pile, this should run down the longer length of the fabric)
- Matching thread
- 15–20 g ($^1/_2$–$^3/_4$ oz) polyester toy filling
- Black embroidery thread

**For the clothes**
- A piece of yellow polyester or nylon fabric (such as that used for lightweight raincoats), measuring 25 x 38 cm (10 x 15 in)
- Matching thread

## TOOLS

- Access to a photocopier or a sheet of tracing paper and pencil
- Scissors
- Sticky tape
- Dressmakers' pins
- Water-soluble pen or quilter's pencil
- Sewing machine (optional)
- Sewing needle
- Embroidery needle

## TO MAKE THE FROG

To begin the Frog, see *Starting a Fleecie Pet* (pages 15–17) for full instructions.

1 To shape the frog's feet, turn up 5 cm (2 in) at the end of each leg and hold in place so that the foot is at a right angle to the leg. Now, using the thread double for extra strength and starting at one of the side seams, work several large, loose slip stitches across the curve at the front of the ankle. To make sure that the finished foot is at a right angle to the leg, the slip stitches will need to pick up fabric 7 or 8 mm (1/4 in) either side of the front ankle crease. Pull up the thread fairly tightly and secure.

2 Mark the position of the frog's eyes, nose and mouth with the water-soluble pen, using the photograph as a guide. With three strands of black embroidery thread, stitch the eyes by working several 5-mm (1/4-in) vertical stitches in and out of the same holes. For the nose, work three of four tiny vertical stitches in and out of the same holes – or you may prefer to use an embroidery stitch called a French knot (see page 11). Add the mouth using back stitch.

3 To mark the frog's fingers and toes, use three strands of the thread you have used to sew the frog (or you can use a matching embroidery thread). The frog's toes should be slightly longer than for most other Fleecie Pets – about 1.5 cm (3/4 in) is ideal. Secure the thread invisibly in the side seam and take the needle out at the starting point for the base of the first finger or toe. Now take the thread over the end of the hand or foot, through the back, and then out through the front, ready to form the next finger or toe. Pull the thread fairly tightly so that it stays in position. Work two more fingers or toes in the same way. Finally, secure the thread invisibly in the side seam.

# To make the raincoat

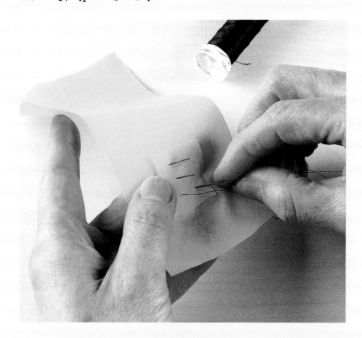

1 Photocopy or trace the raincoat front and back templates, on page 91–92 and cut out one back and two front pieces from the yellow polyester or nylon fabric. Remember that the raincoat has a right and left side so you will need to cut one front piece using the template the right way up and the other using the template face down. (If you fabric is identical on both sides, you do not have to do this.) Cut out two 2 x 2.5 cm (³/₄ x 1 in) pockets and baste in place on the coat fronts, as shown on the template, using a few large running stitches. Machine or hand stitch round the sides and bottom.

2 With right sides of the fabric together, sew the two fronts of the raincoat to the back at sleeve and side seams, allowing a 5-mm (¹/₄-in) seam allowance. Turn the raincoat the right way out.

3 To make the belt, cut out a 2.5 x 25 cm (1 x 10 in) fabric strip. Fold the two long outer edges of the strip of fabric towards the centre so that they overlap slightly and press in place firmly using your fingers or nails to mark the crease. Stitch down the centre of the belt using a machine zigzag stitch or hand running stitch.

TIP If the belt seems too fiddly to make, you could use a 25 cm (10 in) length of narrow polyester ribbon instead.

# Fleecie Pet Accessories

Once your Fleecie Pets are complete, why not adorn them with some specially designed accessories? All the accessories are quick and easy to make, mostly from knitting wool or fleece fabric. And, as they only need small amounts of wool or fleece, they are an ideal way to use up the leftovers from your projects and you can choose to make them in colours that complement your Fleecie Pet's main outfit.

## Knitted poncho

**You will need**
- Small amount (approximately 10g/¹/₂ oz) of double knitting wool in your chosen colour
- Pair of 3.75 (US 5) knitting needles
- Tapestry needle for tassels

**Note:** the poncho is knitted in one piece from the front point to the back point.

Cast on 3 sts. Beg with a k row, k1, inc1, k1, inc1, k1 (5 sts).
Next and every alt (wrong side) row until poncho divides for neck shaping, k2, p to last 2 sts, k2.
**Next row** k2, m1, k1, m1, k2.
Continue in this pattern, making 1 st either side of centre st on k rows (right side) until there are 21 sts, ending with a p row.
**Next row** k10, cast off centre stitch, k to end.
Next and every p (wrong) side row until neck shaping on this side is complete k2, p8.
Turn and continue working on left-hand side of poncho

only, leaving other sts on needle.
Work in st st with garter border for 12 more rows, ending with a p row.
Break yarn and rejoin to neck edge on the p (wrong) side on the other side of the poncho.
Work 13 rows in st st with garter stitch border to match other side, ending with a p row.
**Next row** k10, inc1 into 1st stitch of first side worked, k to end (21 sts).
Next and every p (wrong) side row until 5 sts remain, k2, p to last 2 sts, k2.
**Next row** k8, ssk, k1, k2tog, k to end.
Continue in this pattern, decreasing 1 st either side of centre st on the k (right) side until 5 sts remain, ending with a p row.
**Next row** ssk, k1, k2tog.
Cast off remaining 3 sts and secure loose ends.
You can leave the poncho plain or add tassels. The tassels are made in the same way as those on the scarf (see page 77). Make tassels at the end of every three rows along the outer edges of the poncho.

> **TIP** To work the decreases on the back of the poncho, check out the information given on abbreviations (see page 13) to make sure you understand how to work the 'slip, slip, knit' stitch.

## Woolly hat

**You will need**
- Small amount of double knitting wool in your chosen colour
- Oddment of contrasting double knitting wool to make your pom-pom
- Pair of 3.75 (US 5) knitting needles
- Tapestry needle

Cast on 32 sts in your main colour.
Beg with a k row, work 12 rows in st st, ending with a p row.
**Next row** k2 tog 16 times (16 sts remain).
**Next row** p2 tog 8 times (8 sts remain).
**Next row** k2tog 4 times (4 sts remain).
Cut your wool leaving a 15-cm (6-in) 'tail'. Using a tapestry needle, thread the tail through the remaining 4 sts and pull securely. Use the tail to sew the back seam of the hat (see page 12). Secure ends. The bottom edge of the hat will naturally roll up slightly to form the brim. Make a small pom-pom – about 2 cm (³/₄ in) in diameter by winding a length of knitting wool 20 times round a ruler or 3-cm (1¹/₄-in) wide piece of stiff card. Slip the wool off and tie very tightly round the middle with another piece of wool. To finish, cut the wool loops, trim into shape and stitch in place on top of the hat.

**Tip** If you prefer, you can finish off your woolly hat with a readymade pom-pom. Simply tie the pom-pom round the middle with a piece of standard sewing thread and stitch in place.

## Knitted cape

**You will need**
- Small amount (approximately 10g/¹/₂ oz) of double knitting wool in your chosen colour
- Pair of 3.75 (US 5) knitting needles
- Crochet hook size 4mm/US size 6
- 2 beads for ends of ties (optional)

**Note:** the cape is knitted in one piece from the neck point to the lower edge.

Cast on 24 sts, leaving a 30-cm (12-in) tail of wool to make one of the cape ties.
K 4 rows.
**Next row** k5, inc 1 into next 2 sts, k10, inc 1 into next 2 sts, k5.
**Next and every p row** k2, p to last 2 sts, k2.
**Next k row** k6, inc 1 into next 2 sts, k12, Inc 1 into next 2 sts, k6.
**Next k row** k7, inc 1 into next 2 sts, k14, Inc 1 into next 2 sts, k7.
**Next k row** k8, inc 1 into next 2 sts, k16, Inc 1 into next 2 sts, k8.
**Next k row** k9, inc 1 into next 2 sts, k18, Inc 1 into next 2 sts, k9.
**Next k row** k10, inc 1 into next 2 sts, k20, Inc 1 into next 2 sts, k10.
**Next row** k2, p to last 2 sts, k2.
K 4 rows.
Cast off loosely. Work a 10-cm (4-in) chain of crochet stitches with the tail of wool at the neck edge to make one of the neck ties. Work a matching chain for the other side of the neck and secure in place. (For information on crochet chains, see page 14.) If you would like, finish the neck ties with a bead at each end and knot to keep in place.

# Knitted scarf

**You will need**
- Small amounts of double knitting wool in two contrasting colours
- Pair of 3.75 (US 5) knitting needles
- Tapestry needle

Cast on 5 sts in your first colour.
K 2 rows.
Join second colour and k 2 rows.
Continue in garter stitch in this pattern of stripes until the scarf measures 28 cm (11 in), ending with two rows of your first colour. Cast off and secure loose ends.

To make the tassels, thread the two ends of a short piece of knitting wool through your tapestry needle. Take the needle through a stitch in the cast on or cast off edge of the scarf from the back of your work to the front so that the strand of wool forms a loop on the back of your work. Now take the thread over the edge of the scarf and through the loop. Pull up fairly tightly and trim. Work four more tassels in the same way. Trim the tassels to about 1.5 cm (¹/₂–³/₄ in) long.

# Woolly leg warmers

**You will need**
- Small amount of double knitting wool in your main colour
- Oddment of contrasting knitting wool for the stripes
- Pair of 3.75 (US 5) knitting needles
- Tapestry needle

Cast on 18 sts in your main colour.
Work 4 rows in st st.
Join contrasting colour and work 2 rows in st st.
Rejoin main colour and work another 6 rows in st st.
Join contrasting colour and work 2 rows st st.
Rejoin main colour. Work 4 rows in st st. Cast off loosely.
Join back seam of leg warmer (see page 12) and secure loose ends.
Work another identical leg warmer to complete pair.

---

**NOTE FOR KNITTED ITEMS**

For information on knitting techniques, including abbreviations and piecing together, see page 12–13.

## Fleece jacket

**You will need**
- Piece of fleece in your chosen colour measuring 15 x 34 cm (6 x 13 in) (if the fleece has an obvious pile, this should run down the shorter length of the fabric
- Matching thread

Create a simple jacket by making a fleece sweatshirt like Joe the Monkey's (see page 46), omitting the star appliqué, and simply cut it down the centre. If you wish, you can also add pockets which you can stitch in the same way as those on Leapy the Frog's raincoat (see page 71).

## Fleece scarf

**You will need**
- Oddment of fleece in your chosen colour

Cut out a piece of fleece measuring 28 x 2 cm (11 x ³/₄ in). Make four 1.5 cm (⁵/₄ in) snips along both shorter ends to form a fringe.

## Fleece courier bag

**You will need**
- 2 pieces of fleece each measuring 5 x 5 cm (2 x 2 in) and a 16 x 1 cm (6¹/₄ x ³/₈ in) strip of fleece for strap
- Matching thread
- Decorative button

Place the two pieces of fleece together, fleecy sides (right sides) outwards. Sew round the sides and base of the bag using small running stitches, about 4 mm (¹/₄ in) from the outside edge. To complete the bag, stitch the strap and decorative button in place.

## Fleece waistcoat

**You will need**
- Piece of fleece in your chosen colour measuring 13 x 22 cm (5¹/₄ x 9 in) (if the fleece has an obvious pile, this should run down the shorter length of the fabric
- Matching thread

Create a simple waistcoat by making a tunic top like Hoppy the Rabbit's (see page 41), omitting the flower appliqué and simply cut it down the centre. If you wish, you can also add pockets which you can stitch in the same way as those on Leapy the Frog's raincoat (see page 71).

# Fleece mittens

## You will need
- Oddment of fleece in your chosen colour
- Matching thread
- Length of narrow ribbon (approximately 22 cm/ 9 in) (optional)

Photocopy or trace the mitten template on page 94 and cut out four pieces. Place two pieces together, fleecy sides (right sides) outwards. Hand stitch round the mitten using tiny running stitches, about 2 mm ($^1/_{12}$ in) from the outside edge, leaving the straight edge open for the Fleecie Pet's hooves or paws. Work another identical mitten to complete the pair. If you would like your mittens on a ribbon to make sure they don't get lost, simply sew them to each end of a length of narrow ribbon and thread them through the sleeves of the Fleecie Pet's coat or sweater.

# Fleece pixie hat

## You will need
- Piece of fleece in your chosen colour measuring 15 x 20 cm (6 x 8 in)
- Matching thread
- Small bell

Photocopy or trace the pixie hat template on page 94 and cut it out. Place the hat template on the reverse side of the fleece, making sure that any obvious pile runs down the length of the hat and cut out 1 piece. Fold the hat in half lengthwise so the fleecy sides (the right sides) of the fabric are together. Machine or hand stitch the back seam of the hat, allowing a 5-mm ($^1/_4$-in) seam allowance. Turn the hat the right way out and complete the hat by sewing a small bell on the tip.

Tip For most of the small fleece items, such as the bag and mittens, you will get a much neater result if you sew them by hand as they can be difficult to keep in place on a sewing machine.

Tip When cutting out small shapes from fleece, you will find it much easier if you use a pair of small, really sharp scissors, such as those sold for embroidery.

## Angel wings

### You will need
- 2 pieces of white organza fabric each measuring 16 x 10 cm (6¹/₄ x 4 in)
- Matching thread
- A piece of thin polyester wadding measuring 16 x 10 cm (6¹/₄ x 4 in)
- Water-soluble pen or quilter's pencil

Photocopy or trace the angel wings template on page 94 and cut it out. Place the template on the right side of one of the organza pieces and draw round it in water-soluble pen but do not cut out. With the water-soluble pen, add the small lines coming into the centre of the wing from the edges of the wing curves, as shown on the template. Sandwich the polyester wadding between the two layers of organza. Sew round the wing shape and over the lines, following the marks of your water-soluble pen. Trim the wings very close to the stitched edge and dampen to remove pen marks. Fasten the angel wings to your chosen Fleecie Pet's top, using a few small stitches.

## Necklaces, bracelets and trinkets

You can easily make your Fleecie Pet a choice of necklaces and other items using a variety of beads threaded onto thin elastic or natural cord. Alternatively, you can make a simple necklace by tying a short length of some of the beaded braids that are now available. Marabou feather trims make beautiful boas while readymade ribbon roses and other small trimmings available in haberdashery and craft shops can be used on all manner of outfits. (Remember that buttons, beads and other small extras should not be used on any Fleecie Pet that is being given to a child under three years old.)

## Tags

You may like to complete your Fleecie Pet with a personalised tag, particularly if you are giving it as a gift. To do this, carefully cut out a 6 x 4.5 cm (2¹/₂ x 1³/₄ in) rectangle in thin card in the colour of your choice. Make a hole at the top with a small hole punch or large needle and thread through a piece of thin ribbon or cord. Add details on the label such as your Fleecie Pet's name and the date you created it. If you are giving your Fleecie Pet as a gift, you may also like to include a personal message to the lucky recipient. Finally, use a small safety pin to attach the label to your toy.

# The Fleecie Pet Workshop

Once you have become familiar with the techniques used to make the toys in the book, you'll be ready to start creating your own unique Fleecie Pets. You can do this, of course, by making your toys in different colours and mixing and matching their outfits. But you can also take the idea further. All the toys featured on these pages have been made using the basic Fleecie Pet body and head shapes, clothes and accessories and adding a few clever twists and embellishments.

## Christmas greetings

For Christmas, why not create a troupe of seasonal performers? Santa bear's fur trim is made from a thin piece of white fleece and the rabbit elf's collar is a circle of red fleece, shaped round the edge. The belts are made from cord or ribbon. Rudolph's antlers are brown pipe cleaners which have been shaped, poked into the fabric just behind the centre head seam and secured with a tiny blob of fabric glue. His bright red nose is a readymade 12-mm (1/2-in) pom-pom.

## It's a dog's life

By changing the length of the ears and adding spots, stripes and muzzles, you can create a range of dogs to suit all tastes.

## Family business

You can produce Fleecie Pets in different sizes and even create a whole family of one animal by simply reducing the size of the Fleecie Pet and clothes templates on a photocopier. The rabbit offspring shown here have been made by reducing the templates to 80% and 70% of their original size to create two different sized children. Some of the clothes are a bit fiddly to make if they are too small, so it's a good idea to stick to the more basic items, like those shown.

## Go wild

Design your own breed of Fleecie Pet by combining the basic body with a slightly altered head. The friendly-looking lion shown here has been made using the bear head template and adding a colourful woollen mane. The panda has also been made using the bear template. Before making up, the black ears and white face were seamed in place. The eye patches were added after the toy was stuffed. Other animals you may want to create include a racoon, wolf or wild cat.

## Get personal

For a special gift, why not dress your Fleecie Pet in its own mini version of your relative's or friend's best loved outfit or their favourite sports team?

## Spitting image

Pet lovers everywhere deserve their own Fleecie Pet replica of their favourite pet. This cute bunny is the absolute double of my family's rabbit – but a lot less hard work to look after.

## Strike a pose

By threading pipe cleaners through your Fleecie Pet's limbs while you are stuffing it, you can create a toy that you can bend into a wide variety of poses.

## Exotic creatures

Create your own fantasy beasts by combining bright fleeces with silky sheers and shimmering stretch velvets. The dog's stretch purple suit and the turquoise rabbit's tutu are both made like Patches the Dog's swimsuit (see page 18). For the tutu, a length of wide pink organza ribbon has been gathered along one edge to make the skirt. A small piece of glittery braid has been added round the waist and a readymade ribbon rose completes the outfit. The pink bear's silver halter neck is made like the option given for Squealy the Piglet's bikini top (see page 27).

# Templates

All templates actual size

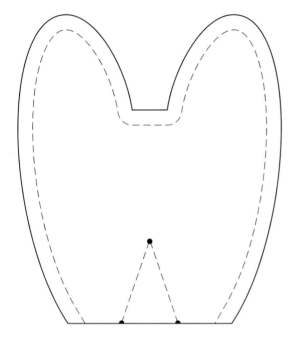

*Patches the Dog face (see pages 18–21)*

*Patches the Dog swimsuit (see pages 18–21)*

*Patches the Dog armband (see pages 18–21)*

*Patches the Dog eyepatch (see pages 18–21)*

*Patches the Dog leg patch (see pages 18–21)*

*Fleecie Pet body (see pages 15–17)*

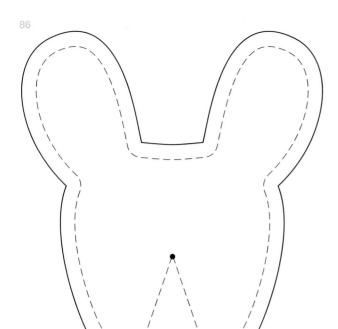

*Sniffy the Mouse and Scrounger the Rat face (see pages 22–26 and pages 60–64)*

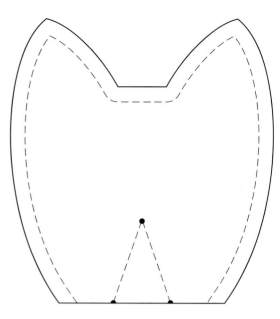

*Squealy the Piglet face (see pages 27–31)*

*Squealy the Piglet bikini shorts (see pages 27–31)*

*Squealy the Piglet bikini top (see pages 27–31)*

*Bruce the Koala face (see pages 32–36)*

*Bruce the Koala vest (see pages 32–36)*

*Bruce the Koala fish appliqué (see pages 32–36)*

*Bruce the Koala shorts (see pages 32–36)*

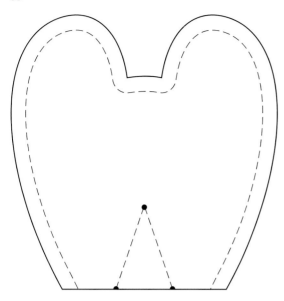

Snowy the Polar Bear Cub and Rumble the Bear face
(see pages 37–40 and pages 56-59)

Snowy the Polar Bear Cub heart appliqué
(see pages 37–40)

Snowy the Polar Bear Cub dress front/back (see pages 37–40)

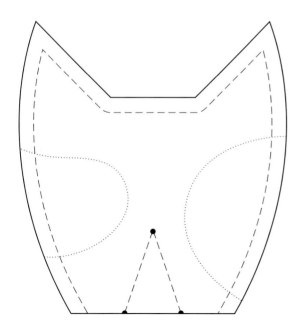

Spangles the Cat face (see pages 51–55)

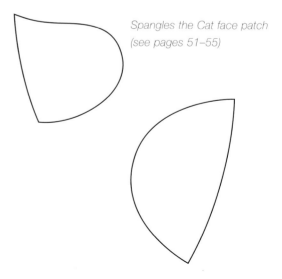

Spangles the Cat face patch
(see pages 51–55)

Spangles the Cat face right patch
(see pages 51–55)

Hoppy the Rabbit face (see pages 41–45)

Hoppy the Rabbit tunic top front/back (see pages 41–45)

Hoppy the Rabbit tunic flower appliqué (see pages 41–45)

Joe the Monkey sweatshirt front/back (see pages 46–50)

Joe the Monkey head (see pages 46–50)

*Joe the Monkey sweatshirt sleeve (see pages 46–50)*

*Joe the Monkey sweatshirt star appliqué (see pages 46–50)*

*Joe the Monkey face (see pages 46–50)*

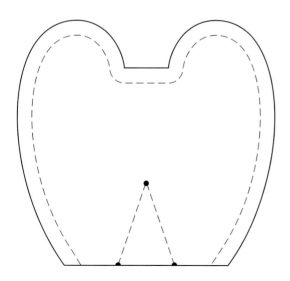

*Leapy the Frog face (see pages 71–74)*

*Fuzzy the Sheep face (see pages 65–70)*

*Hoppy the Rabbit; Joe the Monkey;*
*Scrounger the Rat and Fuzzy the Sheep*
*trousers (see pages 41–45; 46–50; 60–64*
*and 65–70)*

*Fuzzy the Sheep and Leapy the Frog coat front (see pages 65–70 and 71–74)*

*Fuzzy the Sheep coat pocket (see pages 65–70)*

*Fuzzy the Sheep and Leapy the Frog coat back (see pages 65–70 and 71–74)*

*Rumble the Bear dungaree bib*
*(see pages 56–59)*

*Rumble the Bear dungaree legs (see pages 56–59)*

*Rumble the Bear dungaree straps*
*(see pages 56–59)*

*Rumble the Bear dungaree*
*pocket (see pages 56–59)*

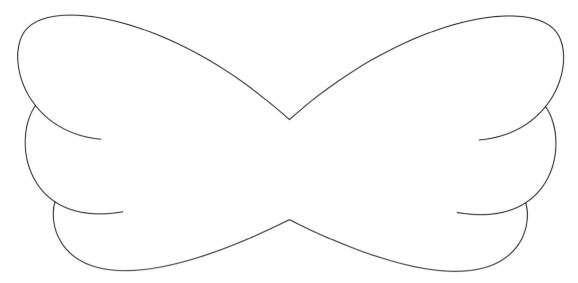

*Angel wings (see page 80)*

*Fleece mittens (see page 79)*

*Fleece pixie hat (see page 79)*

# Suppliers

## MAIL ORDER AND INTERNET SUPPLIERS

### FABRIC LAND
Telephone 01425 461444
Email sue.fabricland@tiscali.co.uk
Website www.fabricland.co.uk
*Fabric (including fleece) and haberdashery. Telephone orders and internet orders accepted. Fabric Land also has 10 retail branches throughout the south of England.*

### FABRIC UK
Registered office:
Carlton Business Centre
Saltley Road
Birmingham B7 4TH
Telephone 0870 350 1936
Email kbt@fabricuk.com
Website www.fabricuk.com
*Fabric (including fleece) and haberdashery. Telephone orders and internet orders accepted.*

### PLANET FLEECE
Website www.planetfleece.co.uk
*Fleece and haberdashery. Internet orders only.*

### THE COTTON PATCH
1285 Stratford Road
Hall Green
Birmingham B28 9AJ
Telephone 0121 702 2840
Email mailorder@cottonpatch.net
Website www.cottonpatch.co.uk
*Wide range of patchwork fabrics and haberdashery items.*

### MAVIS LTD
44 High Street
Bushey
Hertfordshire WD23 3HL
Telephone 020 8950 5445
Website www.mavis-crafts.com
*Wide range of knitting wools and knitting accessories. Available by mail order, internet order or at the shop.*

## RETAIL OUTLETS

### BOROVIK FABRICS
16 Berwick Street
London W1F 0HP
Telephone 020 7437 2180
*Wide range of fabrics including fleece, cottons and speciality fabrics, available at the shop only.*

### THE CLOTH SHOP
14 Berwick Street
London W1F 0PP
Telephone 020 7287 2881
*Wide range of fabrics including some fleece, cottons and speciality fabrics, available at the shop only.*

### FABRIC WAREHOUSE LTD
Packet Boat Lane
Uxbridge
Middlesex UB8 2JP
Telephone 01895 448465
Email enquiries@thefabricwarehouse.com
Website www.thefabricwarehouseltd.com
*Wide range of fleece and other fabrics, and haberdashery items available at the shop only.*

### HOBBYCRAFT GROUP LTD
Telephone 0800 027 2387 for details of local stores
Website www.hobbycraft.co.uk
*28 stores in England and Wales with wide range of haberdashery items, knitting wools and patchwork fabrics. Call for details of your nearest store or see website.*

### JOHN LEWIS PARTNERSHIP
Head Office:
Partnership House
Carlisle Place
London SW1P 1BX
Telephone 020 7828 1000
Website www.johnlewis.com
*Haberdashery and knitting wools. Some stores also sell fabrics. Stores throughout England and Scotland. Phone for details of your local store or look on the website.*

# Index